KITTEN

HOW TO USE THIS BOOK

Read the captions in the eight-page booklet.
Using the labels beside each sticker, choose the
kitten that best fits in the space available.

•

Don't forget that your stickers can be stuck down
and peeled off again. If you are careful, you can
use your kitten stickers more than once.

•

You can also use your kitten stickers to make
your own book, or for school projects.

First American Edition, 1996
14 16 18 20 19 17 15 13

Published in the United States by
DK Publishing, Inc.,
375 Hudson Street
New York, New York 10014

ISBN 0-7894-1347-7

Reproduced by Colourscan, Singapore

Printed and bound in China by L.Rex Printing Co., Ltd.

LONDON, NEW YORK, MUNICH, MELBOURNE, DELHI
See our complete product line at
www.dk.com

Curious kittens

Play is a very important part of a kitten's development. If it has brothers and sisters to play with before it is seven weeks old, a kitten is likely to grow into a confident and strong cat. Through games, kittens learn how to hide, fight, and hunt. Playing teaches them how other kittens will react to their movements, and helps them form friendships with their owners.

Growing up
By the time a kitten is about seven weeks old, it can balance and walk like an adult, and it can hold and grip objects. This kitten is calmly investigating a toy – it will soon be able to hunt alone successfully.

Early advantage
Kittens that don't have the chance to play during the early weeks of their lives are more likely to grow into unsociable, quiet cats. Those with brothers and sisters develop quickly, learning by watching and playing together.

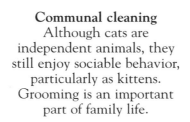

Communal cleaning
Although cats are independent animals, they still enjoy sociable behavior, particularly as kittens. Grooming is an important part of family life.

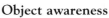

Object awareness
These kittens are becoming aware of the objects around them. By watching the way things move, and by following the noises they make, kittens learn about the connections between sound and movement.

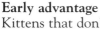

Head-to-head
A cat shows friendship by rubbing its head against its owner or other animals. Kittens first do this in play, and quickly develop relaxed head-to-head contact habits.

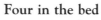

Four in the bed
Kittens are most active early in the morning and late at night. They regularly doze during the day after energetic play. As they get older, they will prefer to sleep alone.

Fearless friends
Most animals feel very exposed lying on their backs. Young kittens don't have such fear, and they enjoy the comfort and security of human contact.

In training
This kitten is practicing a "bird swat." It is too young now to reach properly, but soon it will leap into the air to catch its prey.

Gripping power
At eight weeks, kittens have full control over their paws and can grip and carry things. Once they have learned to hold objects, they may become possessive like a small child, and refuse to share their toys.

Mirror, mirror
Kittens have pupils that grow very large in the dark and very small in bright light, regulating the intake of light by which they see. Although they cannot see any better than humans, they are far better at working in the dark.

Hide and seek
All kittens have a natural curiosity, and at around three weeks, as their confidence improves, they begin to explore. They will climb and hide inside things, learning about their surroundings and their own bodies.

Entertaining a friend
While this kitten is young, it is curious about other animals. The position it is sitting in indicates that it isn't scared, nor will it hurt the frog. Meeting other animals at this age means it will be well-socialized when older.

Starting to stalk
Kittens have developed hunting behaviors by about the age of five weeks. They start to stalk each other after about three weeks, and objects soon after that.

Forever young
By keeping cats as pets, we ensure that they always have enough food, warmth, and companionship. They don't need to develop the same independent habits they would in the wild, and will happily play like kittens even when fully grown.

Body talk
Cats have very graceful and agile bodies. Their skeleton is designed to help them jump, pounce, and balance well. Kittens start to use their full range of movements when they are about four weeks old.

Full examination
This kitten is mimicking its mother's behavior and smelling its "prey" before tasting it. The mother has taught her litter to investigate things through smell, touch, and taste.

Various breeds

There are many types of kittens, in hundreds of colors, sizes, and lengths of fur. Some kittens look completely different than their parents. There are more than 100 pedigree cat breeds, and many more non-pedigree, produced by parents of different breeds. These kittens can have characteristics of both parents, so each one in a litter may be slightly different.

Mix and match
This kitten had a Blue-cream Shorthair mother, and a Blue Shorthair father. Its brothers and sisters could be either pure cream, or blue, or a mix.

Points of color
This is a color-point kitten, which means that it has areas of darker fur on its face, ears, legs, feet, and tail. The points can be many different colors, from brown and silver to blue.

A unique pet
These kittens are crossbreed kittens – their parents were different breeds. Non-pedigree kittens inherit various characteristics from their pedigree parents, and can combine the best characteristics of both.

Show kitten
These are friendly Brown Classic Tabby kittens. In a show, judges look for orange eyes and a brick-red nose in this breed.

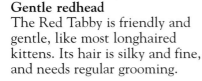

Gentle redhead
The Red Tabby is friendly and gentle, like most longhaired kittens. Its hair is silky and fine, and needs regular grooming.

Elegant Asian
This tiny kitten is a Singapura, bred from the feral cats of Singapore. The kitten's coat gets shorter in appearance as it gets older, and its eyes change from green to blue.

Dual nationality
This kitten is an Asian Red Cornelian, although the breed was developed in Britain. Cornelians are lively, friendly kittens with fine, short hair.

Oriental family
These are Oriental Chocolate Spotted kittens, sitting with their grandfather. This breed is descended from Siamese cats. The kittens have a solid line down their spines, but this should become spotted as they grow.

COLORS AND MARKINGS

A startling ginger kitten

A rare white tiger cub

A patchy tortoiseshell and white kitten

A playful tortoiseshell kitten

Unusual Chocolate and Lilac Shorthairs

A Blue and White British Shorthair

A distinctive, spotted Bengal Leopard

A Cinnamon Angora with her three kittens

A Blue-gray Chartreux

A pale Birman kitten with her mother

A Blue Spotted British Shorthair

A Birman kitten with a black-tipped Burmilla

Creamy Siamese kittens

A blue and cream crossbreed

A deep brown Chocolate Shorthair

LONGHAIRED

Longhaired Birman kittens

A ginger kitten
learning to socialize

Brown Classic Tabby kittens

A Ragdoll charmer

A beautiful, thick-coated Silver
Tabby and her kitten

A young
Silver Tabby

A Red Tabby

A litter of curious
Birman kittens

A Silver Shaded
Persian kitten

A Persian hunter

Tabby and ginger
crossbreeds

A blue-eyed
Cinnamon Angora

A Birman baby

A Blue-cream Persian

Blue and white
crossbreed kittens

SHORTHAIRED

A catnapping
tortoiseshell

An elegant
Singapura
kitten

A hungry
cream tabby

Crossbreed kittens
playing hide and seek

A tiny brown
tabby

A blue and
cream cross-
breed kitten

A playful
Oriental kitten

A young
puma cub

A cream color-point
kitten

Blue and Cream British
Shorthairs

A balancing
tortoiseshell

A domestic
relative of
the African
Wild Cat

A ginger with an
unusual friend

A curious Asian
Red Cornelian

A flexible Siamese kitten

KITTEN LIFE

A playful
tortoiseshell tabby

A five-week-old
tabby kitten
grooming

A tabby nursing
her litter

Shorthaired
Oriental kittens
exploring

A Siamese kitten
staying close to
mother

Newborn kittens
huddling together

Tabby and tortoiseshell
kittens exploring the
litter box

A contented
tabby kitten

A prowling
tiger cub

A wide-eyed
young cream
kitten

A Blue-cream
Persian lapping
milk

A basket of
sleepy tabbies

Birman
playmates

A watchful
leopard cub

A six-day-old tabby
snuggling with its
mother

Dark chocolate
Chocolate Shorthairs are not common, but they are calm, friendly cats, and make excellent pets. While they are kittens, the tabby markings are very clear.

Birman legend
The very first Birman is said to have been a white temple cat. When the temple's head priest lay dying, it rubbed its paws and face against him – everywhere it touched him, its fur turned a darker shade.

Clever camouflage
There are many different types of tabby patterns, found on both domestic pets and wild cats. The spots and stripes provide excellent camouflage and can help a cat hide and hunt effectively.

Floppy kittens
Ragdoll kittens make ideal family pets. They become very limp and relaxed when they are picked up, which is how they got their name, and they love being stroked and fussed over.

Shining example
While young, Silver Tabby kittens are often mainly black, with just traces of silver. They are among the most beautiful of cats when fully grown with silver coats.

Lovely Angora
Litters of the Cinnamon Angora are rarely smaller than three kittens. These Angoras have long, triangular heads, sharp ears, and fine, silky fur. They make friendly and playful pets.

French pedigree
This sturdy kitten is a Blue-gray Chartreux. Legend says that this friendly French breed was developed by monks in a monastery near Grenoble in the 1300s.

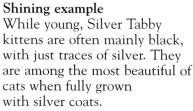

"Spotties"
Cats with spotted markings date back as far as ancient Egypt. This is the Blue Spotted British Shorthair. Although the spots aren't all the same size, they show up plainly.

Color confusion
This Silver Shaded Persian kitten is very similar to a Chinchilla kitten. In fact, if these kittens become paler in color as they get older, they are called Chinchillas.

Kitten care

A kitten is blind and helpless in its first nine days, and usually stays with its mother to be fed and protected until it is about nine weeks old. A kitten learns all its basic skills and habits by watching its mother. Once it is old enough, a kitten is happy to live with a human family.

Manhandled
Kittens do not always enjoy being picked up. They need to feel relaxed and secure, so cradle them carefully.

Sibling rivalry
The constant rivalry for food and attention in a large litter means that the kittens tend to be alert and active. They should grow into playful, curious, and lively cats.

Head to tail
A kitten learns how to wash itself by watching its mother. Kittens are naturally very clean animals, and grooming is instinctive when a kitten is relaxed.

Basic training
A kitten should be litter trained early on. Cats are fussy about smells and texture, so once they are happy using a litter box, it is best not to change the type of litter.

Scratch and sniff
Smell and taste are important senses for a young kitten. Smell is the first to develop, and the most useful when investigating.

Well groomed
Longhaired kittens need regular grooming to prevent their coats from becoming matted. Most cats enjoy being brushed – it feels similar to being licked by their mother.

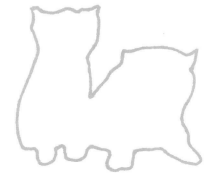

Family connections
A kitten learns the scent of its mother very early and associates it with comfort and security. It will keep coming back to her for protection as it starts to explore.

Powers of concentration
These kittens are focusing on a toy. They have learned that if they look away, it may move. This is instinctive hunting behavior, which is often shown in play.

6

Bath from mother
Being groomed by its mother not only teaches this kitten how to keep itself clean, it also strengthens the bond between the mother and the kitten. Kittens begin to clean each other as they get older for the same reason.

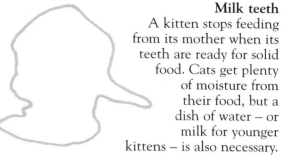

Milk teeth
A kitten stops feeding from its mother when its teeth are ready for solid food. Cats get plenty of moisture from their food, but a dish of water – or milk for younger kittens – is also necessary.

Comfort food
These kittens don't need their mother's milk anymore, but feel comforted by staying close to her, as if they were still feeding.

Touching behavior
Petting your kitten every day ensures that it will grow up enjoying the company of humans. It also helps the kitten feel secure without its mother.

Central heating
These kittens are huddled together to keep warm while their mother looks for food.

Making progress
At just three weeks, a kitten can support its body and walk, although its balance is poor. By the time it is five weeks old, all its senses and its balance are fully developed.

Professional sleepers
Kittens will always look for warm, secure places to sleep. They sleep for about 16 hours a day, almost twice as long as most other mammals.

Early learning
Kittens develop curiosity earlier than fear, so a mother's role includes keeping them out of trouble. Until they are about six weeks old, she is their guardian in more ways than one.

Natural caretakers
Fostering is a natural instinct in cats, developed so that while one mother hunted, another would nurse her litter. Cats will happily accept orphaned kittens into their litter if they have just given birth.

Wild kittens

There are wild cats all over the world. They are not pack animals, and usually like to live alone once they are adult. Wild kittens, or cubs, have to grow up quickly, learning to defend themselves and hunt for food early on. Cubs often have fur colorings or patterns that provide camouflage, both to protect them when young, and to help them hide when hunting. All domestic kittens are descended from small wild cats such as the African Wild Cat, and there is even evidence that cavemen kept pet cats.

White beauty
The striking white tiger was once a familiar sight in northern and eastern India. There are now only a few left. Its color comes from a white gene similar to that found in domestic cats. White tiger cubs have very large feet and look clumsy until their bodies catch up in size.

Under threat
Leopard cubs are cared for by their mothers until they are about two years old. As adults, they are agile climbers – they will often take food up into a tree for safety before eating. Leopards, like many other animals, are decreasing in number rapidly. Humans hunt them for their fur, and are also destroying their natural habitat.

Spots and stripes
The puma is similar to a domestic cat, and even purrs like one. Although the cub is marked with spots, these merge to form the stripes of an adult puma.

Burning bright
The tiger is the largest and most powerful of all cats. It needs a great deal of meat to survive, so it is a skilled hunter. The tiger is an endangered species, and cubs are especially vulnerable until they are independent.

Asian hunter
The Bengal Leopard is a domestic pet, developed from the Asian leopard. Its coat is very distinctive and similar to a leopard's. This kitten is friendly and gentle, and its fur is now the only thing that ties it to its wild ancestry.

A friendly wild cat
This non-pedigree blue and white kitten is directly related to the African Wild Cat. The Victorians used cats like this one to breed the British Shorthair. When breeding pedigree cats from cross-breeds, the cats are chosen for certain qualities, such as their color and temperament.

Scrapbooking

Projects

"Bad to the Axle"

Contents

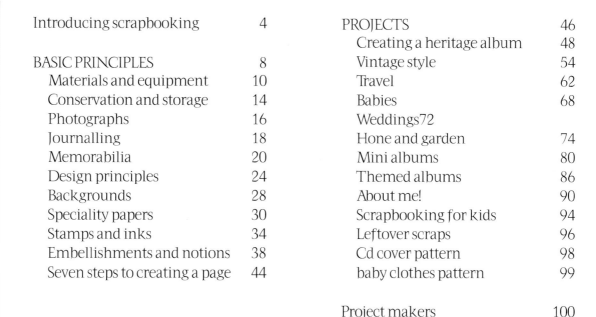

Introducing scrapbooking

Modern scrapbooking is a rapidly growing craft geared at teaching the preservation of photographs and capturing life's significant moments through words or 'journalling'. The art of scrapbooking combines the principles of photograph preservation with the principles behind the design of an appealing layout.

HISTORY

Scrapbooking began several hundred years ago, when people used diaries, journals and hand-made albums to record thoughts, recipes, poetry and quotes. The earliest surviving book dates from the seventeenth century in Germany.

Throughout history, artists and other creative thinkers have kept scrapbooks of drawings, ideas and text. Among them was the great Renaissance artist and scientist, Leonardo da Vinci. Amazingly,

many of his pages have been the inspiration for today's printed papers, vellum and rubber stamps.

References to 'common-place books' appear as early as the 1590s. These included collections of diary entries, drawings and newspaper clippings.

Even Shakespeare's play *Hamlet* mentions the recording of notes in a commonplace book. In 1706, the British philosopher John Locke published his *New Method of Making Commonplace Books*, which advises readers on the best way to preserve ideas, proverbs, speeches and other notes. By 1825, the term 'scrapboook' was in use and a magazine devoted to the hobby, *The Scrapbook*, was in circulation.

In the late nineteenth century, scrapbooks attained popular status and many magazines published ideas on what to include in them. Mementos, such as newspaper clippings, pressed flowers, calling cards, letters, ribbons and locks of hair, all found their way into personal scrapbooks. Pictures were etched or engraved onto the pages.

During the Victorian era, even more embellishments were added to scrapbook pages, such as ornamental vignettes and cut-outs. Die-cuts (pre-cut paper shapes) and stamps were introduced in the 1870s and companies manufactured images specifically for inclusion in these albums.

In the late nineteenth century, the invention of the camera added a new dimension to the art of scrapbooking. As photography became more widespread and affordable, photographs began to appear in scrapbook albums.

During the 1880s, an increased focus on the study of genealogy–the identification and preservation of family roots–gave scrapbooking another new direction. This fascination continues today as many families research their genealogies as a means of discovering connections to the past and preserving the family heritage for the future.

Today's scrapbooks may vary greatly from those of the 1500s. The manner in which they are presented and preserved has evolved, reflecting the knowledge of preservation and archival techniques. However, one common thread connects the past to the present–scrapbooks have always told a story.

SCRAPBOOK OCCASIONS

Many scrapbookers begin with a particular event in mind: a baby is born, or someone in the family is getting married, starting school, having a significant birthday, graduating, retiring or experiencing hard times, such as the death of a loved one. Once a goal or reason has been established, it is time to sort through photographs and memorabilia, organizing them and then ordering them to tell a story.

The great thing about scrapbooking is that anyone can do it. The only prerequisites are being able to cut and paste. This craft appeals to all age groups. Children love to get involved and kids can scrapbook.

The creation of a scrapbook can bring families together as they share highlights and rekindle memories. Children enjoy looking through family scrapbooks, especially when events meaningful to them are scrapbooked and journalled.

Scrapbooking the difficult or sad times, like divorce, death, moving, or any major change in the family structure, can even help children and adults. The pages of the scrapbook, with patterns made from colours, shapes and textures, emphasize that life is an imperfect but dynamic mixture of events and emotions.

A scrapbook can be created for any theme: a year album, baby album, heritage album or school album. Albums can also display an individual's collections, such as cars, teacups, teddy bears, quilts, letters or postcards.

Many businesses, from florists to restaurants, use scrapbooks to showcase their various products and services.

Albums can be created as special gifts, such as mini brag (baby) books, kitchen tea (recipe) collections, wedding anniversary and birthday books.

The beauty of this craft is that there is no right or wrong. Scrapbooking should be a meaningful experience for the creator, free from judgment or critique.

The selection of photographs, papers, embellishments and journalling should reflect the scrapbooker's own personality and their taste.

Modern scrapbooking is a communal pastime. Scrapbooking shops often support groups of scrapbookers by providing access to shop equipment. Scrapbookers derive the practical benefit of sharing costly equipment, such as punches and tools, as well as finding inspiration and mutual interests. It's also a great way to make new friends.

The ideas and techniques shared in this book will provide the beginner or experienced scrapbooker with the inspiration and knowledge to create a wonderful album, filled with mementos for the family and future generations.

Basic

Principles

Materials and equipment

When you are first assembling your scrapbooking materials you will start with the most basic cutting and pasting tools, but the scope of the craft is so wide that a fantastic range of materials and equipment can be utilized in the creation of each page. Specialist products are available from scrapbooking stores.

PAPER

All paper used for scrapbooking should be acid and lignin free. Cardstock is a thick, sturdy paper that can be used to hold all the elements of a page together. Printed paper tends to be thinner. Photographs are either directly mounted (attached) onto cardstock or matted (adhered to layers of paper) first, then mounted. Cardstock is available in more than 400 colours and numerous textures. Printed papers also come in a wide variety, including hearts, animal prints, floral, lace, water, checks and stripes.

As current scrapbooking trends have originated in the USA all sizes for scrapbooking are in inches. The most common paper size is 12 x 12 inches or 30.5 x 30.5 cm. Other sizes are available, such as 8 1/2 x 11 inches or 21.5 x 27 cm, but selections in patterned papers are somewhat limited.

ADHESIVES

Any adhesive used in a scrapbook must be acid free. Some adhesives allow for items to be shifted, others set quickly.

Options include glue dots, bottled glue, glue sticks, liquid glue pens and silicone glue. Photo tape has a peel-off backing and double-sided tape comes on a tape roller. Adhesive photo corners are useful.

A good choice for a novice scrapbooker is the double-sided tabs that come in a box or dispenser. The advantage is that they are refillable and cost effective.

Glue sticks are great for children, due to ease of use and reasonable pricing.

The choice of adhesives also depends on what is being attached, its size and weight. Fabric is best attached with an acid-free craft glue (PVA). Silicone glue is great for tiny items but heavy items such as pockets or foam core require strong glues.

PENS

A pen or marker used in a scrapbook must be of archival quality, waterproof, fade resistant, non-bleeding and acid free.

Pens used in scrapbooking are made from pigment ink; therefore the ink is permanent. When starting, a good-quality black pen with a monoline nib is essential for journalling.

There are several varieties of pens available. These include monoline, calligraphy or chisel point, brush, scroll, and gel pens. There is also a red-eye pen that is used for removing the red from people's eyes in photos.

The Vanishing Ink Pen is filled with special ink that will vanish off the pages within 24–72 hours. It is a great alternative to the lead pencil as it will not leave any stray marks.

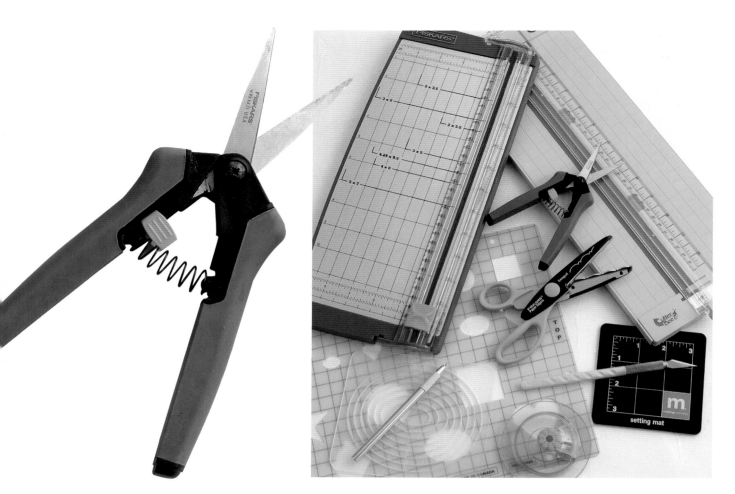

CUTTING TOOLS

Scissors are used extensively in scrapbooking so purchasing a sturdy, sharp pair of paper scissors will prove to be a valuable investment.

Every scrapbooker should also invest in a paper trimmer. A 30.5 cm (12-inch) paper trimmer is recommended as it will provide a sufficient cutting surface for an entire sheet of the standard 30.5 cm (12-inch) square cardstock. There are many different brands on the market today. The most versatile paper trimmers have an extension ruler and a few different types of blades for scoring and for perforating.

Fancy scissors are often used to create different edges. They can be purchased in a wide variety of styles.

Cutting systems have also been developed to help in cutting shapes like circles and ovals. Many of them can cut a variety of shapes as well as letters of the alphabet.

PAGE PROTECTORS

It is important to place completed pages directly into a page protector to prevent people touching and damaging the material. Once people see the completed pages they will be eager to look through them over and over again. Keeping pages protected will ensure that photographs and papers will be free from fingerprints and dust as well as acids from handling.

It is important that page protectors be made from polypropylene, polyethylene and polyester plastics. Always avoid any products made from PVC as they will be harmful to photographs.

Events featured in scrapbooks often require more than a double-page spread, so expanding page protectors are a suitable option. These will also allow for more memorabilia to be included in the layouts.

Special pocket pages are available for featuring and protecting memorabilia.

TYPES OF ALBUMS

The most popular album size is 30.5 x 30.5 cm (12 x 12 inches), but smaller sizes are also available. There are three main types of albums: three ringed, strap-hinged and post-bound.

Three-ringed binders are easy to use, hold more pages and are often cheaper than other types of albums. Completed pages are inserted into page protectors that can be easily moved.

Strap-hinged albums allow the book to expand to the length of the strap. Facing pages lie flat, enabling continuity in a double-page spread. The albums usually come with a white background page. Page protectors for these albums can be side-loading or top-loading.

Post-bound albums are expandable, with the addition of extra posts. Pages in post-bound albums can be easily moved around and arranged. Page protectors for these albums are top-loading.

Conservation and storage

Scrapbooking is all about preserving memories for generations still to come. Scientific knowledge regarding the conservation of paper, photographs and other materials has given the modern scrapbooker a distinct advantage. This craft now provides a safe, archival means of storing and displaying treasured photographs.

DETERIORATION

In recent decades, attempts to store and display photographs have unwittingly led to their destruction. Magnetic albums or albums with plastic coverings made from polyvinyl chloride (PVC) were used to keep precious photographs safe. Unfortunately, the materials in these albums contained chemicals that, with time, break down to form acids. These acids, in turn, begin breaking down any adjacent papers or photographs. The scientific term for this is acid migration.

Many papers contain lignin, a chemical compound derived from plant matter. In time, lignin will also break down causing the paper to yellow and become brittle. The process of deterioration affects surrounding material such as the paper and any photographs with which it is in contact.

REMOVING PHOTOGRAPHS FROM OLD MAGNETIC ALBUMS

Keen scrapbookers will want to take measures to salvage precious photographic material from old magnetic albums.

The process for removing photographs is simple, but requires some care. A blow-dryer should be held about 12 cm (5 inches) away from the album. The heat from the blow-dryer will help to soften the glue.

Dental floss can then be used behind the photographs to lift them without damage to these treasures. If this does not work, an acid-free product called Un-Du can be used. Simply put a few drops into the scoop and apply carefully underneath each photograph. The photographs should lift easily without any ensuing damage.

RESTORATION

Once photographs are removed from old albums a quick inspection will reveal if there has been any damage caused by the PVC covers and acids.

Replicate any photos that are in danger of deterioration. This can be done by scanning or reprinting photos or even making colour photocopies on acid-free paper as a temporary solution.

Damaged photographs can be restored in many different ways. Professional photo labs provide restoration services for photographs and negatives.

Extremely old photographs and photographic plates should be assessed by specialist restorers.

SCANNING

Photographs can also be scanned at home on a quality scanner. The scanned image can then be manipulated using a photo software package. Images of photographs scanned at home can be saved onto a floppy disk or CD-ROM as a JPEG or TIFF file, then taken to a professional lab for developing. This will avoid wear and tear on a printer.

A new generation of scanners has recently emerged and these will automatically restore damaged photos as they are being scanned.

Technology has placed the tools that were once limited to a few specialists in the hands of every scrapbooker.

NEGATIVE STORAGE

Negatives and slide film should always be stored away from photographs. It is suggested that negatives be placed in polyester or polypropylene plastic sleeves to ensure that they will be free from any damage caused by acid migration.

Not all negative sleeves provided by photo developers are acid free, so take a little time to organize their storage.

Once negatives are stored properly, they will last for years, allowing scrapbookers to reprint photographs that may be decades old.

Professional photo labs are constantly upgrading their services. Quality, old negatives can actually be reprinted with better colour saturation and brightness than in their original printing.

CONSERVATION TERMS

Acid The chemical property of a material with a pH level less than 7.0

Acid free The make-up or chemistry of materials that have a pH level of 7.0 or higher

Archival quality A description of materials that are permanent, durable or chemically stable, and are suitable for preservation

Lignin A compound found in paper derived from plant matter. It is the part of the plant that gives it strength and rigidity

Photographs

Photography is the key element of modern scrapbooking. The ordering and labelling of photographs form the scrapbook's story. Organizing photograph collections, rather than saving them for a rainy day that never arrives, is essential. After all, who wouldn't appreciate having a well-prepared photo album from generations ago?

PHOTO DATING TIPS

It can be difficult to sort photographs into years as many people do not record this information on the back of photographs. However, these factors will help make it easier to identify the year or approximate date in which a photograph was taken.

- Age of the people
- Fashion
- Furniture
- Cars
- Hair styles
- Travel, holidays
- Homes lived in
- Schools attended

SORTING

The best way to start organizing years of photographs is to first move all the photographs, albums and memorabilia to one location in your home. Once a comfortable spot (that doesn't need to be cleared at dinner time) has been established, you can sort through the photographs. The easiest way to sort is in chronological order, working backwards from today.

Clear off a large work area and grab some stick-on notes to label each year. As photos are being sorted they can be placed into the corresponding year group. Once this is completed the next step is to revisit each pile and re-sort the photographs into months or events.

LABELLING

Unfortunately, too many people have collections of old photographs in their homes that have been passed down through the generations without any identifying details. Often, these details are lost forever as the people who may remember names, dates and locations are no longer living.

As the sorting process is taking place, record any information related to the photographs to ensure that all relevant information is captured, such as who is in the photo, when it was taken, and its location. The sorting process often rekindles memories and feelings associated with the past, so make the most of any reminiscences by recording them.

Use a soft graphite pencil to write on the back of photographs. Do not use a ball-point pen or lead pencil as they can damage the photographs.

CHRONOLOGICAL ORDER

A set of photos labelled and sorted into chronological order is the starting point for a scrapbooker's collection. Simply record the year on the front of each box then place the photographs in order.

If there are several photos of the same event, in lieu of writing on the back of each one, use a journalling card to record all the information relating to that event. Once the recording is complete, place the card in the box in front of the photographs.

Journalling cards make scrapbooking a particular event easier as they provide all the details at a quick glance.

THEMES

As photographs are being sorted into chronological order, themes will begin to emerge. This is a great place for the novice scrapbooker to start. Decide on a particular theme and then gather photos. This theme could be a recent holiday, house renovation or family celebration.

As a beginner, it is advisable to save wedding, baby or heritage photos for scrapbooking at a later time as these are the most precious photographic resources. The results should reflect the care and creativity that your heirlooms deserve.

Scrapbooking skills will improve with knowledge and experience. This book will provide the appropriate techniques to develop your skills and to scrapbook valued photographs with confidence.

PHOTO STORAGE

Photo boxes are an ideal storage solution when sorting photographs into chronological order. However, make sure the photo boxes are made from acid-free cardboard.

Take the time to add in the journalling cards as it will save time and energy when planning the layouts.

Store the photo boxes in a cool, dry location to avoid any damage from light or mould.

Journalling

Journalling is the creation of titles, headings and text on the scrapbook page. It is one of the most important aspects of modern scrapbooking. It records important facts, dates and recollections that might otherwise be forgotten. Journalling also tells the wonderful stories behind the pictures–it allows a scrapbook to come to life!

JOURNALLING TIPS

An easy way to remember the kind of information to include in scrapbooks is to think of the five Ws:

Who is in the pictures? Record the first and last names, especially of the people who are not part of the immediate family.

What was happening?

When did it happen? Always include the date somewhere on your page.

Where did it happen? Include as much detail as possible such as addresses, restaurants, signs, buildings and landmarks

Why did it happen? Explain the whole story.

THE ART OF JOURNALLING

Photographs can capture and record many memories, but those memories are not complete without words.

Journalling is really about what you would like to say if you were talking someone through your photo album. People tend to explain the story behind photographs. Scrapbook journalling needs to do the same. Of course journalling may just provide facts and dates, but it can also set the tone or scene for an album.

Journalling styles can be humorous, sentimental, informative or highly personal–or all of the above!

The decision about what to write in a scrapbook depends heavily on the type of album being created, its audience and the personality of the individual scrapbooker.

RECORDING THE PAST

To help the process of recalling details, jot down notes on a personal calendar or a notepad. Journalling cards for photo boxes are a great way to stay organized. If writing on the back of photographs, always use a graphite pencil or a removable stick-on note.

When journalling for a scrapbook it is recommended that a separate sheet of paper be used, which is cut and mounted on the layout. This will prevent any costly mistakes.

Do not fret over the quality of your handwriting! The content is actually more meaningful than the appearance of the letters. Handwriting carries the characteristics of an individual's personality, making its preservation very special. Even if the computer is used for text within an album, every effort should be made to include some samples of handwriting.

JOURNALLING THE FAMILY

When journalling, it is interesting to gather input from the people present in the photographs. Getting family members involved will make the reading much more fun and more precious in years to come. Remember to incorporate the handwriting of other family members.

Writing fond sentiments about friends and family in a journal entry is a great way to capture feelings and thoughts that will live on. As albums are revisited over time, the reading of journal entries will build and strengthen relationships.

Occasionally, people find themselves at a particular event with no camera to capture the notable moments. When there are no photographs for a particular event, it can still be successfully scrapbooked through journalling or by using other memorabilia. This will allow a record to be kept of an occasion that, in time, might otherwise be forgotten.

HIDDEN JOURNALLING

Occasionally the journalling included in a layout is of a personal or sensitive nature and is not intended for everyone's viewing. In these cases, consider applying some hidden journalling techniques.

Journalling can be placed in envelopes or flaps that are attached to a layout. A journalling entry can also be tucked behind photographs or other embellishments on a page.

Other more elaborate options include putting the journalling on pull-out tags, a mini-book or even a CD.

Hidden journalling can also be attached to the back of a layout, keeping its contents secure.

JOURNALLING THE HARD TIMES

Journalling the difficult times in life will help sort out thoughts and emotions related to the event. In many cases recording them can help family members in the healing process.

Events like death, illness, divorce, natural disasters, fires, floods and cyclones should not be avoided in a scrapbook. Their presence will emphasize that life is not perfect, but rather a mixture of events and emotions all responsible for moulding a family's dynamics.

Memorabilia

Memorabilia is a record of items worth remembering. It can be anything that provides information on or permanent evidence of a past event. To scrapbookers memorabilia can be just as important as photographs. Highly effective layouts can be created simply with journalling and pieces of memorabilia.

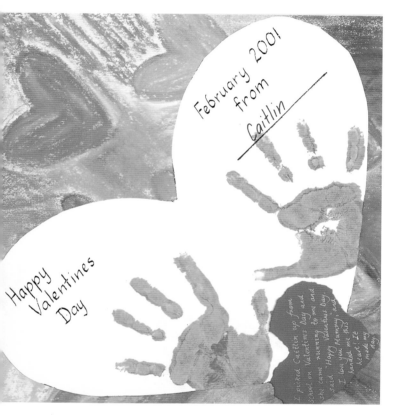

WHAT TO KEEP

Use memorabilia to tell a story, just as you would use a photograph. Journalling can describe the details as well as the feelings associated with scrapbooked memorabilia.

Childhood memorabilia will be treasured in years to come. Cards, letters, paintings, projects and stories from school can be scrapbooked and journalled. If the original artwork is fragile, photograph it and scrapbook the photograph. Items such as the first missing tooth, or handprints that depict a child at a particular age of development will be especially meaningful.

When photographs are not available for a particular event, memorabilia, along with journalling, can still form a dynamic layout. Knowledge of this should help free every scrapbooker from any limitations when it comes to creating a layout for any occasion or theme.

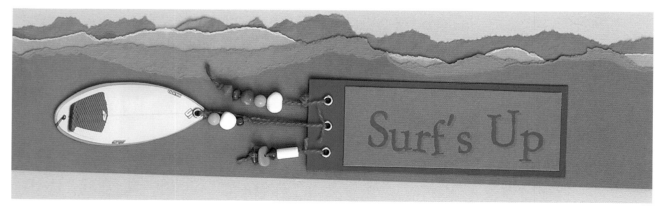

MEMORABILIA PRESERVATION

When using original paper items, such as certificates or letters, be sure to de-acidify them with a de-acidifying spray (available from craft stores) prior to including them on a layout. These sprays, such as 'Archival Mist', contain an alkaline buffer that will neutralize any acid that is present in the paper.

Newspaper articles should be photocopied onto acid-free, lignin-free paper. They can also be sprayed with a de-acidifying spray and laminated.

Most fabrics are safe in your scrapbooks since natural fibres do not contain acid.

The Xyron laminating and sticker-making machine can protect organic items like flowers. The laminate is acid free and see through. However, do not laminate any items that may have a future use. Do not use ultrasound photos with a heated laminating machine.

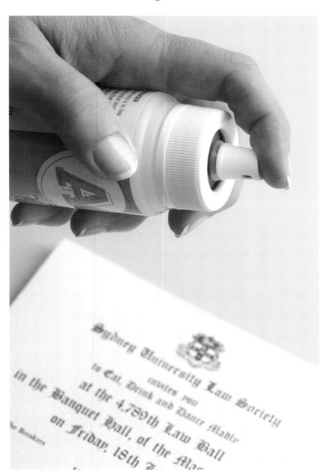

STORING ORIGINALS

Another effective alternative is to first scan items and then reprint them onto acid-free, lignin-free paper.

If the items are especially valuable, consider scrapbooking colour copies and storing the originals in acid-free envelopes. Remember to store them in a safe place, free from humidity or direct sunlight.

Occasionally scrapbookers come across items that would be meaningful in a scrapbook but are too bulky or large for a layout. The alternative is to photograph each item. Then the photographs can easily be incorporated onto a scrapbook page and provide a permanent record in the event that the item is lost or no longer available in the future.

Items like furniture, cars, paintings and quilts can often be damaged, passed on, or sold in years to come so this will keep their place in a family's history.

MEMORABILIA TIPS

Following are some suggestions for memorabilia to keep:

Babies: ultrasound photos, hospital bracelets, baby booties, corner of a favourite blanket, swatch of fabric from the christening dress, lock of hair, first rattle, first bib

Vacations: maps, travel brochures, business cards, menus, postcards, hotel stationery, ticket stubs, foreign coins and notes, receipts, postage stamps

Home: cards and letters, paint swatches, house plans, old keys

Family favourites: handkerchiefs, charm bracelets, buttons, tie clips, hair clips, pocket watches, brooches, doilies, rings

Records and awards: certificates, ribbons, scout badges, ID cards, report cards, medals, diplomas.

MEMORABILIA KEEPERS

Memorabilia should be removable from a scrapbook page just in case it is required at some time in the future.

Self-adhesive photograph corners enable quick removal of memorabilia and look effective on a scrapbook layout.

Another option is plastic memorabilia holders. They have an adhesive backing that can stick onto a page in seconds. They also have a flap that can be opened and closed for easy access. Memorabilia holders come in variety of sizes and are great for hair clippings, sand, jewellery, tiny shells, pressed flowers and small coins.

Clear plastic page protectors with pockets for memorabilia, such as coin collector pages, are available in different shapes. These are great for storing thin 3-D memorabilia such as coins, jewellery and dried flowers and memorabilia that is double-sided.

POCKETS AND FRAMES

Pocket pages are useful for storing larger items of memorabilia. They can be created by the scrap-booker in any shape or style and designed to complement and enhance the theme of a layout.

Vellum is especially useful for pocket pages because it is translucent and allows the item to be seen.

Acid-free, double-sided tape is the best adhesive for pocket pages. Pockets can also be attached with eyelets or brads or sewn with fabric and thread for an impressive presentation.

Raised frames, such as box frames, also make attractive memorabilia keepers on the scrap-book page.

Design principles

Scrapbooking applies the design principles used by photographers and graphic artists. You can easily achieve an effective layout after spending some time practising these basic rules. Individual creativity is the extra ingredient that will make each design your own.

BASIC LAYOUTS

Before beginning the actual page layout process, ask the following questions: What is the goal or theme of this layout? Who is the layout for? What feelings should this layout evoke? The next step is to determine the focal point. In scrapbooking the focal point is usually a photograph; however, it can also be a journalling item, piece of memorabilia, or an embellishment that emphasizes the theme of a page. Since the focal point is the first place the eye catches, proper placement is critical. Often a photograph can be enlarged or cropped to achieve emphasis. Matting is another effective way to establish a photo as a focal point. Double or triple matting a photograph will naturally draw attention. Framing will also draw the eye to the focal point.

Late **May**, Mum and Dad were on their **Honeymoon** in Italy. They spent about three weeks **touring** various locations and visiting relatives. On this particular day they were exploring Mum's birthplace in **Naples**. Earlier in the week they had partially climbed **Mount Vesuvius**. Of course Mum wore her dress and heels. A few days later they took a ferry ride across the **Bay of Naples**. With the wind blowing through her hair and the picturesque scenery in the background, Mum had captured the **classic** look of the day.

In those days Mum hardly wore any make-up. She was and still is a **natural** beauty. The gentleness captured in these photos is a **reflection** of her personality we all **love** and **admire**.

Although she left **Italy** when she was only four, she quickly recaptured the essence of her **heritage**. It was as if she had never left. Mum and Dad had a great time on their Honeymoon. Of course, Mum's **smile** captured everyone's **heart** in Dad's family. Dad had truly picked a real **gem**.

BALANCE

The first rule of creating a great layout is achieving balance. In a balanced layout all the elements are arranged so that the entire layout has a consistent visual weight. If a layout is unbalanced it will cause the visual flow to be affected, diminishing the value of some photos. Artists often turn their canvases upside down to check for balance. This technique actually works well for the scrapbooker. It will direct the eye to the unbalanced portion, which can often be easily corrected by a slight adjustment or addition. Embellishments such as charms or die-cuts, could provide the necessary element for balance.

RULE OF THIRDS AND 'Z' MOVEMENT

The rule of thirds is a technique that has been used by artists and photographers for decades. Applied correctly, it can help to achieve an effective layout with visual appeal. Usually applied to rectangular pages it works just as well on the standard 30.5 x 30.5 cm (12 x 12 inch) page. The rule divides the page into thirds both horizontally and vertically, creating nine smaller sections and four points of intersection. Placement of the most important elements on the intersections will create a visually effective layout.

Creating a 'Z' movement on a page is another great technique. This is achieved by arranging elements so that they form a 'Z'. This guides the eye naturally through the page from left to right, then down, creating an appealing flow.

SHAPES

Geometric shapes are visually appealing and add flair to any layout. While cropping a photograph can add shape and interest, extensive cropping is not recommended.

Cutting a sharp corner with a circle can soften a feature but still provide emphasis. Devices such as punches and decorative scissors provide a quick method of shaping elements on a page.

Embellishments can also quickly add shape to a layout. They include circular, rectangular and square tags, stickers, metals, buttons and charms.

COLOUR

Colour is the predominant element in a page design. It has the ability to dictate the entire mood. Colours are categorized as either warm or cool. Purples, blues, and greens inspire feelings of tranquillity and peace. The warm colours–reds, yellows and oranges–evoke energy and playfulness. The depth of colours can also affect the tone of a layout. Deep, dark colours suggest a regal atmosphere while light, pale colours imply a delicate, soft feel. Earthy tones are appealing as the colours are neutral and do not compete with other tones in the photos.

Colours in a layout should either complement or enhance the focal point in the photo grouping. There are a few colour schemes that can be followed. The monochromatic scheme uses one colour selection in different shades. A complementary colour scheme uses colours that are found on the opposite sides of a colour wheel. The triadic colour scheme selects three colours of the same value. This means they must be all soft, bold, muted, light or dark. Finally, the split complementary colour scheme utilizes one colour from the photo and one or more complementary colours. Experiment with these schemes, duplicating a few good photos so that layout options can then be compared.

Less is more with colours. Try a limit of three colour choices with a ratio of 60 per cent dominant colour, 30 per cent complementary colour and 10 per cent additional complementary colour.

Backgrounds

Create backgrounds for your scrapbooking page by selecting a piece of cardstock or printed paper that co-ordinates with your photographs. You will find the easiest way to make an appropriate choice of paper is to have your photographs with you to get a good match. The most difficult procedure is choosing from the amazing variety of papers that are available.

USING PATTERNED PAPER

Patterned paper can potentially add personality to a scrapbook page. It can reflect the theme or nature of an event. The whole piece can either be used as the entire background or cut into smaller pieces to make a more complex background for the page.

INSPIRATION FROM PHOTOGRAPHS

Backgrounds for a page can also be created by utilizing elements within the photographs. Themes from photographs can be extended into the background as well. This may be as easy as selecting a paper that matches or re-creating an element from the photographs in the background. When re-creating an element from the photos look for something small, such as a pattern from an item of clothing, or an architectural element.

COLOUR BLOCKING

The colour-blocking technique is actually what the name suggests. It involves arranging two or more block shaped (square or rectangle) pieces of paper of complementary colours to build a geometrically patterned background. Colour blocking is a quick way to add impact to a page (refer to the layout entitled My First Set of Wheels).

Colour-blocked pages are simple to create and often do not require additional accents–just some favourite photos. Experiment with colour blocking and try varying the size and number of blocked areas. Practise using different colour combinations, but make sure your colours support rather than detract from the photographs. Colour-blocking templates make this technique even easier. Simply use the template to indicate where the colour-blocked pieces should be placed.

Venice

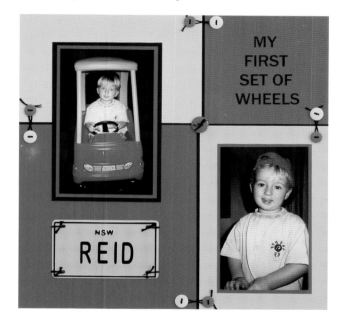

PATTERNED PAPER TIPS

Try these ideas for using patterned paper backgrounds to enhance your design.

Creating a border Cut or tear a strip of patterned paper for a quick border accent.

Matting photos Photographs can be emphasized with a double or triple mat. The patterned paper can appear as the second layer. Using cardstock against the photograph separates it visually from the patterned paper and further distinguishes it as the focus of the page.

Creating leading lines Cut patterned paper into strips and place them horizontally, vertically or diagonally across the page to direct the eye to a focal point.

Cut out decorative elements from the sheet of patterned paper to provide interest, balance or extend a theme.

Specialty papers

Specialty papers are those that do not fall under the heading of cardstock or patterned paper. Some of the most prized specialty papers include mulberry, handmade and metallic varieties. They come in a wide array of textures and thicknesses and lend extra interest or add special effects to the pages without greatly increasing the bulk.

MULBERRY AND OTHER SPECIALTY PAPERS

Some of the more common specialty papers are handmade, metallic and mulberry. Vellum is another specialty paper used extensively in scrapbooking; this paper is covered in more detail on page 32.

Mulberry is actually a thin, fibrous paper made from the inner bark of the mulberry tree. It is pliable and loosely woven with long fibres. Mulberry paper is often torn to reveal an uneven edge, giving it a soft 'fuzzy' appearance.

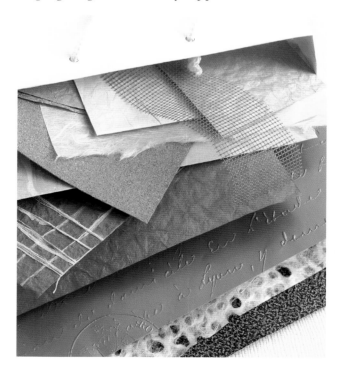

There are many other varieties of specialty papers for scrapbooking, including cork, rippled cardboard, maruyama (thin mesh-like Japanese paper), suede and printable canvas. Always ensure the papers are acid and lignin free before using them in an archival album.

HANDMADE PAPERS

Handmade papers add a wonderful texture and homemade feel to a layout. They come in a variety of colours, patterns and thicknesses.

Some handmade papers are made with leaves and flowers embedded in the fibres for a pretty touch, and some are embossed with patterns.

Handmade papers can be easily made by using leftover scraps of cardstock; paper-making kits are available at most craft stores.

METALLIC PAPERS

Papers that give the appearance of metal in a variety of finishes, such as flat, diamond dust, mirror, pearlescent and iridescent, are known as metallic papers.

Colours range from pastels to silver, gold and black. They are often used as photo mats or cut into smaller pieces for faux-metal embellishments such as photo corners.

Inkjet printers and normal inks will not work well on this paper, so if writing on them, use a quick-drying pen such as a Slick Writer.

1 To create a torn-edge effect on matting made from mulberry paper, use a water pen, cotton bud or small paintbrush dipped in water. Draw a line of water along the paper where it is to be torn. This will help to control the tearing.

3 Allow the mulberry paper to dry completely before adhering the mat to your layout.

2 Gently pull the mulberry paper at the wet edges and the fibres will separate easily.

VELLUM

Vellum is a translucent paper similar to, but thicker than, tracing paper. It is acid and lignin free and comes in a variety of colours, printed patterns and textures. Vellum provides many entrancing options for scrapbookers such as subtley patterned backgrounds, delicately layered matting, gorgeous embellishments and translucent pockets.

Vellum takes its name from the medieval paper it resembles that was made from animal skin. Modern vellums are made from plant products and come in a wide range of colours, patterns and textures.

Select your vellum in conjunction with the background cardstock. Deeper or brighter-coloured backgrounds can be used, as placing the vellum on top will soften or mute the colour dramatically.

If you wish to match the cardstock to a particular photograph, a layer of white vellum on top will mute the cardstock, providing a closer match to the photograph.

Vellum is the ideal choice for making delicate pockets on your scrapbook pages. The translucent quality of the vellum lends elegance to the page while still providing practical storage for memorabilia. See instructions on page 33.

JOURNALLING WITH VELLUM

Vellum can make your journalling easier. In the back of this book you have been given templates for writing fonts. Simply place vellum over the top and trace with your archivally safe pen, then add colour.

Vellum can even be used with a computer printer to great effect. With some printers it helps to use a colour other than black, such as grey, brown or blue, to eliminate the bleeding process.

Print out headings or text on a sheet of paper (A4). This will show exactly where the text will be printed.

Use a removable adhesive to attach a scrap piece of vellum on top of the writing, then refeed the paper through the printer. This is an attractive, economical method for using up scrap pieces of vellum.

ATTACHING VELLUM

Vellum is translucent so most adhesives will show through. However, different techniques can be used to avoid this problem.

If using vellum to mat photographs, start attaching the layers from the top. Any adhesive can be used underneath the photograph without being noticed.

If nothing is being placed on top of the vellum, there are several suitable adhesive products. These include clear-mounting tabs, double-sided tapes and vellum adhesive sprays. The least noticeable is the vellum adhesive spray, which allows the flexibility of repositioning. Access to a Xyron machine provides a big advantage as this machine can transform a piece of vellum into a sticker.

Scrapbook stores also carry a large range of brads, eyelets, snaps, paper nails and conchos that are effective when mounting vellum onto cardstock.

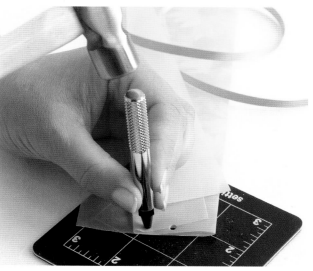

1 Cut out two rectangles of vellum to make a pocket for your layout. Fold each piece in half then make a flap by folding at an angle as shown. The second piece should have a larger flap. Slot the two pieces together.

2 Punch three sets of two small holes into the vellum with a hole punch and hammer.

3 Secure the vellum with two pieces of matching ribbon. Thread each ribbon through the holes and tie it in a knot. Embellish the pocket as desired.

Stamps and inks

Rubber stamping and wet embossing were around long before archival scrapbooking came on the scene. Scrapbookers now use these techniques to create distinctive backgrounds, titles and embellishments. With some knowledge and a dash of inspiration, the scrapbooker can bring a unique dimension to any layout.

RUBBER STAMPING AND EMBOSSING

In the past, keen 'stampers' confined their craft mainly to cards and papercraft. However, as scrapbookers are always seeking new innovations for layouts, rubber stamping and embossing are now a feature in many scrapbook albums.

The layouts in this section have all been enhanced with a rubber stamping or embossing technique. These techniques take little time, but are very effective.

Experiment with different techniques and do not be afraid to try new things. Make each layout

a work of art by incorporating different media.

However, before adding rubber stamping and embossing to cherished layouts a scrapbooker must become knowledgeable about the different stamp pads and their uses.

DYE INK PADS

Dye ink pads are water based and dry quickly on all types of paper.

These pads are acid free, permanent and sometimes waterproof, if indicated on the cover.

Dye ink pads come in a large assortment of colours. However, as the dye ink dries it becomes lighter and slightly muted.

It is recommended that scrapbookers purchase brands that are labelled archival, since archival inks are not only acid free, but fade resistant as well.

Dye ink pads are not used for wet embossing. However, they can be applied directly on paper to create a beautiful multicoloured background.

Use light-coloured dye ink pads with shadow stamps to create subtle backgrounds for titles, headings, adornments or journalling blocks.

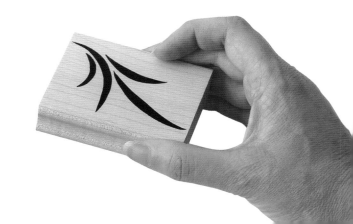

PIGMENT INK PADS

Pigment ink pads produce sharp and striking impressions. They provide rich, saturated colours that work well with embossing.

Pigment inks come in a wide range of colours and are acid free and fade resistant. It is recommended that clear embossing powder be used with pigment inks. However, a pigment ink can be applied without embossing as long as it is given adequate drying time.

Since pigment inks are made from particles of pigment, they work best on non-glossy paper, especially in the absence of embossing powder.

Drying time may vary, especially with metallic inks, so a heat gun may be used to set the colour. Simply hold the heat gun above the impressions and move it along in an even manner. This will help the colour set into the paper.

SPECIALTY INK PADS

Metallic inks are pigment inks that often require heat setting. They offer more vibrancy and pearlescence than the standard pigment pad. However, many of these pads are not child safe and some are not archival or acid free.

Recently, metallic inks that work well on all types of media and do not require heat have appeared on the market. Check labels carefully for details.

Specialty pads, such as VersaMark, provide a watermark effect on paper (see the step-by-step instructions on page 37). These create wonderful backgrounds and can be used in conjunction with chalks and Pearl Ex products.

A new product called StazOn ink can be used on a large range of surfaces like plastic, metal, glass, ceramic, laminated paper, coated paper and leather. It is a fast-drying, solvent ink that provides flexibility when creating works of art.

EMBOSSING PADS

Embossing pads can be clear or have a slight tint that makes it easier to see an impression's placement before applying the embossing powder.

These pads are used only for wet embossing. Once applied on paper, embossing powder must be added, then heated to create a beautiful raised image.

Embossing powders come in a large assortment of colours and a few textures. Images with fine details usually require fine embossing powder for a crisp image. However, not all rubber stamps are suitable for wet embossing. Suitability is determined by the texture, grain and detail of the rubber stamps.

Often rubber stamps created from images of photographs can only be used with dye-based ink and some pigment ink pads. It is suggested that some time be spent experimenting before deciding on the best ink pad for a rubber stamp.

ALPHABET STAMPING TIPS

Alphabet sets come in different sizes and styles and can be used with every type of ink pad.

Use a set of alphabet stamps for titles, tags and other embellishments.

Use a negative alphabet stamp for eye-catching titles.

Stamp letters onto a strip of paper and then cut them out for a more interesting tiled effect.

EMBOSSING TOOLS

Embossing pens are an invaluable addition for any scrapbooker.

Embossing pens can be purchased in an assortment of nib styles and offer the scrapbooker the ability to emboss their own handwriting. These pens are used in conjunction with embossing powders and a heat tool.

When using wet embossing, a heat tool is the best source of heat to set the image.

The heat from a heat tool is extremely hot and, unlike a blow-dryer that blows air, it produces a direct heat that melts and sets the embossing powder. The heat tools can be purchased in a range of styles and sizes.

Heat guns can also be used to shrink plastic that has been stamped or embossed. Read the manufacturer's directions before beginning.

WET EMBOSSING

Wet embossing can transform an ordinary die-cut into a work of art.

In the layout Precious Little One, an ordinary blue die-cut was selected. Colour was added directly to the die-cut from a pigment-based pad. Next, clear embossing powder was applied and set with a heat tool. The process was repeated until just the right look was achieved.

The wet embossing process adds dimension to the die-cut and will naturally create a crackled effect, especially when the process is repeated a number of times.

Plain stickers can be revitalized by applying the embossing ink and then sprinkling clear embossing powder over the image. However, in this instance, the heat tool must be used with caution, since many new stickers are plastic based.

EMBOSSING POWDERS

Embossing powders are available in a wide range of colours. They are to be used in conjunction with an embossing ink pad.

Simply ink the stamp with embossing ink and stamp the image on to the paper. Next, sprinkle on the desired embossing powder colour. Tap off the excess embossing powder. Use the heat gun to set the powder.

Once set, the image will appear raised and bolder in colour.

Printed papers work well with the embosssing powder process and provide a more artistic feel.

EMBOSSED PIGMENT INKS

When pigment inks are embossed they produce a beautifully raised image. The Happy Birthday layout displays this technique.

Since the layout colour was intentionally kept neutral, no further technique was applied to the image. However, once the image is embossed, chalks, coloured pencils, watercolours, and watercolour pens can be applied in order to add dimension and colour.

Using a multicoloured pigment ink pad will add an appealing gradation of colour for added interest or contrast.

1 Choose a simple stamp to form an effective background pattern on solid green cardstock. Ink the stamp with a watermark ink pad such as VersaMark.

2 Stamp the image onto the paper. The colour of the paper will be slightly darkened, creating an eye-catching background.

3 Repeat this process until a cascading pattern is achieved. Leave the background to dry completely before assembling the layout.

Embellishments and notions

Embellishments are all the extras used on a scrapbook page, such as stickers, pressed flowers or haberdashery. Embellishments accent the photographs, add visual interest or texture and can help balance the layout. Scrapbook embellishment also provides craftspeople with the opportunity to showcase their different skills.

EMBELLISHMENT TIPS

The following is a list of embellishments available in good scrapbook stores:

- Eyelets
- Brads
- Threads
- Ribbon
- Lace
- Buttons
- Wire
- Magic Mesh
- Stickers
- Conchos
- Frames
- Fabric
- Beads
- Tags
- Paper clips

Charms
- Slide mounts
- Page pebbles
- Metal letters
- Metal words
- Metal charms
- Pressed flowers
- Washers
- Watch parts
- Keys
- Metal photo
  corners
- Metal engraved
  plates
- Metal rings
- Jump rings
- Woven labels

EMBELLISHING THE PAGE

Embellishments may include stickers, die-cuts, preserved plants, fabric, haberdashery and even small items of hardware. The list is extensive and often reflects the newest trends.

The great thing about scrapbooking is that it gives people with skills in a wide range of crafts the opportunity to display them. Skills such as paper quilling or sewing can be used for embellishing the scrapbook page in a unique and personal way.

Page embellishments can be either strong or subtle. First decide how the embellishment will function. For example, embellishments such as fabric, felt, mulberry and handmade paper will add a tactile aspect to any layout.

Embellishments should reflect the subject matter, so look for links between your photos and different embellishments.

PLACEMENT

If adding embellishments as an accent, experiment with their placement.

Do not limit accents to just filling in an empty space. Place them so they are peeking out from behind photographs, use them to embellish journalling blocks, or cut off an edge to give a more natural, pleasing result.

Use groupings to bring logic to accents; for example, although leaves may look fine randomly scattered throughout a layout, they may actually be more effective if grouped in clusters of three, especially when emphasizing a focal point or journalling block.

COLLECTING NOTIONS

Notions are items of haberdashery that personalize scrapbook pages and add interest. They can add the perfect finishing touch to a layout; choosing what to use and how to use it is all part of the fun of this hobby.

Sewing supply and haberdashery stores are a great source for notions, as are thrift or second-hand stores. Imaginative use of everyday items found in the home will extend your collection of notions even further.

The only limitation to using notions is that they need to be acid-free (as most fabrics are) or sprayed with an anti-acid agent.

Keen collectors of notions will check old clothes for useable parts like buttons or trimmings before throwing them out. Even the fabric itself can often be used.

Notions are often handed down in the family and an old button box is a treasured find for the avid scrapbooker. Old-fashioned buttons and laces look especially lovely on heritage layouts and may themselves be a family heirloom.

RIBBON, LACE AND THREAD

Ribbons and laces are easily acquired and have many uses. Use ribbon for a small bow to embellish a photo mat. Wrap ribbons and lace around the entire layout and tie in a bow to form a pretty border. Trim the edge of a heritage photo mat or journalling box with lace.

Small roses made from ribbon can be purchased ready-made in a rainbow of colours and they make attractive embellishments or borders.

Threads, string and twine are used to tie items to the page. They can also be wrapped around frames or small envelopes. Thread them through eyelets to form borders on layouts and photo mats or use them to hang tags.

A twisted ribbon made from your own combination of different kinds of fibres is a pretty and unique way to embellish a layout with some old-world style.

BUTTONS AND FABRIC

Buttons are a favourite as they sit flat and can be sewn or glued to a layout.

Buttons can be used in a number of ways–as part of the title (such as a small button on top of the letter 'i'), sewn onto the corners of photos and journalling boxes, lined up to form a border or attached to a tag.

Choose fabrics for colour or texture according to the theme of the page. Use darker, rich-coloured fabrics for autumn and winter layouts, lighter pastels for spring and vibrant colours for summer.

Wrap fabric around a photo frame or use a heavily textured fabric (such as hessian) as a photo mat.

Tulle is a lightweight and effective fabric, especially evocative on wedding layouts. Lay a piece of tulle over one corner of the layout or use scraps of tulle to dress up die-cuts.

BEADS, SEQUINS AND GLITTER

Add some sparkle to your scrapbook layouts by gluing glitter or sequins to the edges of a photo mat or journalling box. Thread beads onto wire, pins or thin thread and stitch or glue to a layout element. Beads can also be dangled on a knotted thread from the bottom of a photo mat or title.

TWILL (COTTON TAPE)

Twill or cotton tape is used to tie items together in a bundle. Twill is very versatile as it can be dyed, stamped or imprinted, allowing you to change its colour to match the page.

Most computer printers will allow twill to be fed through easily, provided it is tightly secured to a piece of paper or cardstock.

PINS AND HOOKS AND EYES

Use pins to attach tags to frames or mats. Pins are also good for attaching photos, paper or vellum to a page. Small beads can be threaded onto a safety pin or hat. Metal charms or alphabet letters look great hanging from pins.

Hooks and eyes can also be used to hang items from a frame or mat and as connectors for fibres.

CHARMS AND COSTUME JEWELLERY

Tiny charms, such as hearts, butterflies, flowers, keys or footballs, take on a special meaning when used on an appropriately themed page.

Charms can be tied with threads or fibres, attached with glue, threaded onto a pin or wire and attached with a jump ring or clip.

Broken jewellery or jewellery that is no longer in fashion can add a fun touch and special meaning to pages. Attach smaller jewellery items as you would attach charms.

HINGES

Hinges come in many shapes and sizes and can be purchased from scrapbooking, hardware or craft stores. There are ornamental hinges (such as those used on jewellery box lids) or plainer, heavier hinges to choose from. They can be functional as well as decorative, and are used to create 'doors' on pages. Attach hinges with a strong silicone-based glue or crystal lacquer.

CLOSURES (BUCKLES, D-RINGS, AND CLASPS)

Thread ribbon or twill through a buckle or D-ring to form a closure for a mini-book on a page. Wrap fibres around one side of the page and use a clasp to connect them at the front. Use a small buckle to join two or more ribbons around a photo mat or journalling box.

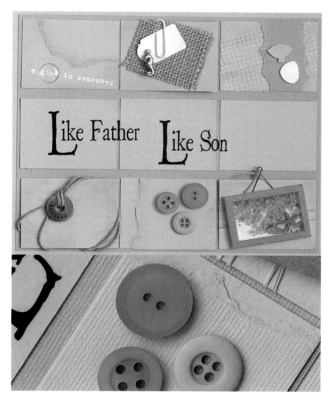

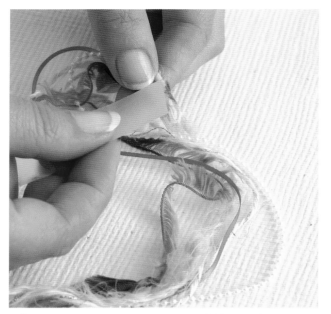

1 Select four different types of fibres of varying textures, such as a pearl string, ribbons and wool. After cutting the fibres to the same length, group and secure them together by wrapping tape around one end.

2 Begin twisting or plaiting the fibres together, starting from the taped end and working down the length. When the twisting is complete, tape the unsecured ends together to prevent the twist from unravelling.

3 Attach to the front of the layout using glue dots or small amounts of silicone glue so the twist is held in place. Wrap the ends over the top and bottom edges of the layout and adhere to the back with tape or glue.

Seven steps to completing a page

1 SELECT A THEME

Select a group of photographs that go well together and clearly tell a story. The number depends on the size of the photographs and the theme. A single large photograph on a page is effective in special scrapbooks, such as a wedding or heritage album.

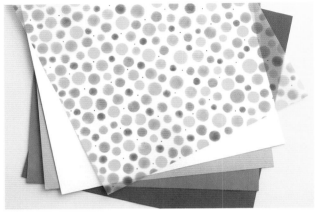

2 CO-ORDINATE PAPERS

Take the photographs with you when purchasing papers as there are more than 400 colours of cardstock and thousands of printed paper designs to choose from. Select different colours and place them behind the photographs to see which combinations work best.

3 CROP PHOTOGRAPHS

Cropping is where some of the photographs are trimmed and cut. Scrapbookers can try inventive or minimal cropping, depending on the quality of the photographs and individual taste. However, do not crop precious or one-of-a-kind photographs.

4 MAT PHOTOGRAPHS

Matting is the piece of cardstock adhered behind the photographs in order to highlight them. The number of layers and the colour choices can vary, depending on the desired impact.

5 LAY OUT THE PAGE

Once matted, lay the photographs out on a two-page spread of cardstock. Re-arrange the items on the page until the desired balanced design has been achieved, then attach the items to the page. Refer to the section on Design Principles for more information.

6 CREATE THE TITLES AND JOURNALLING

Decide on a title or heading and then see how it will be displayed in the available space. The journalling or stories about the layout are very important. Try to record all those details that future generations will find interesting.

7 ADD MEMORABILIA OR EMBELLISHMENTS

Lastly, add any memorabilia that may be relevant to the pictures. If there is no memorabilia, consider adding some type of embellishment that will enhance and complete the layout.

Tiny fingers, little toes,
chubby cheeks and pretty clot

travel

AROUND
the WORLD

Z

is for

Projects

Ruth Godden was a beautiful
Bridesmaid at the marriage of her sister
Elsie, to Eric Norman.

Creating a heritage album

A heritage album is a wonderful way to preserve the past. Creating an album will involve older family members in a unique piece of historical research and provide a fascinating story for younger members of the family. As heritage photos are usually rare and precious, every effort must be taken to ensure their prolonged life for future generations.

HERITAGE TIPS

Use a de-acidification spray to preserve paper documents. This will not repair any past damage, but it will prevent further damage and prevent acid migration to other items on the layout.

Photocopy any newspaper clippings onto acid-free, off-white paper for a more authentic look. Chalking can also age the documents.

Colour-copy one side of a postcard, then attach the original on the page using photo corners. Place the copy next to it on the page, so both sides can be seen at once.

Collect heritage-embellishment products such as tags, frames, vintage writing, reproduced vintage postcards, postage stamps, labels and tickets to use on layouts.

SORTING PHOTOGRAPHS

Before starting to scrapbook a family's heritage album, some time must be spent sorting old photos and memorabilia.

It's always a good idea to have clean hands as fingerprints will cause damage to the photographs.

Begin sorting the photographs in chronological order. If possible, make some time to sit with the oldest-living relative to gain more insight into the photograph's background.

Names of people, places and events will help when compiling the journalling. Possible dates or eras and knowing the relationship connection will bring clarity when creating the album.

This information will also provide some details that may be used to complete a search on the internet or at a local historical society.

PHOTOGRAPH RESTORATION

While sorting the photos, you may find there are many photographs that require restoration. There are several options when restoring photographs. The most professional, and most expensive, finish is provided by a photo conservator.

Colour copiers can be used as a quick option but will not provide optimal results. Other affordable options include using duplicating machines like the Kodak Image Maker Machine, available in many chain stores. They will restore colour and make minor corrections to old photos.

It may take some time and effort, but photographs can be restored using a home computer, quality scanner and photography software. There are numerous software products available that produce professional results.

My Great Grandfather James Albert Gannon with his
second wife Winnie, during WWII

CROPPING

It is not recommended that heritage photographs be cropped. The only time it might be appropriate to crop is when the photograph has torn edges or markings. In this case, use the paper trimmer, sparingly, to remove the unwanted areas.

A better option would be to find a frame that hides the worn areas. Framing can showcase heritage photographs, especially frames in oval shapes.

It is best that you have several copies of heritage photographs to be used for special features. These copies can then be cropped, collaged and altered to create interesting layouts.

The originals can be stored in protective acid-free pockets on the back of layouts.

For more tips on altering photographs or papers, refer to the Vintage Style section of this book.

FAMILY TREES

A heritage album is relatively easy to organize and plan as the number of photographs, memorabilia and details is known prior to beginning.

A great way to start a heritage album is to complete a family tree. The family tree will display the whole family and provide the necessary connections for future reference.

Written names, small photographs or a combination of both may be used to create this type of layout. There are printed papers manufactured with family tree outlines that make the job easier. Specialized computer software programs will create beautiful family trees that can then be printed, cut out and placed on a scrapbook layout.

Use the push-out family tree frames (see the Template section at the back of this book) to create your own family tree. Reduce or enlarge family pictures so the face of the person who is featured will fit inside the frame. This can be done with a colour photocopier or scanner, but always print onto acid-free paper.

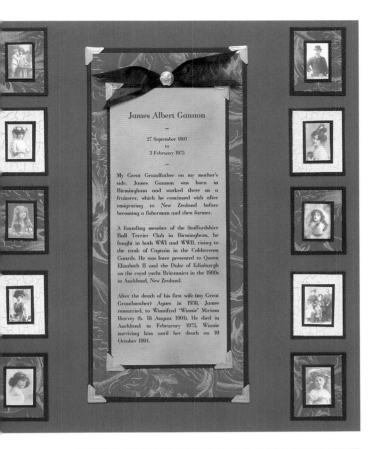

Add glue dots to the back of the push-out frame and secure it to the copy. Write the person's name in the panel and add the framed picture to your family-tree layout.

BACKGROUNDS

Muted background colours are often preferred in heritage albums as they reflect a more vintage feel. A stylish choice is to use particular shades of colour to represent each side of the family, for example, a father's side in shades of blue and a mother's side in shades of burgundy.

ATTACHING ITEMS

Photo corners are a great attachment option for heritage layouts as the items can still be removed if required. Photo corners can also hold memorabilia in place. Photo slit punches work in the same way. Permanent adhesives are not recommended for heritage albums.

MEMORABILIA

Memorabilia can help families connect with the past. Some suggested items for a heritage album are handwritten recipes, old documents such as marriage certificates, fabric from clothing, letters, pins, rings, handkerchiefs, monogrammed items, old lace and crocheted pieces.

1 Select a piece of old cream-coloured lace or a handkerchief and a large sheet of dark-coloured cardstock (A3). Place under a colour photocopier, lace side down. Make copies on large, acid-free copy paper (A3). Don't worry if the lace has flaws as these will add character.

2 Create a frame 30.5 x 30.5 cm (12 x 12 inches) square and about 5 cm (2 inch) wide from matching cardstock. Position the frame over the colour copy, taking into account the features of the lace. Attach the frame with spray glue and trim the copy to fit.

3 Decorate a copy of a heritage photo using cotton lace fixed to the back with glue dots. Make several layers of matching photo mats and embellish the layout with ribbons, dried flowers and charms.

circa 1875

Vintage style

The vintage or deliberately aged look is very popular with scrapbookers because it creates the feel of bygone eras. A wonderful range of ready-made 'shabby-look' products is available from most craft stores. However, there are many ways to achieve the aged look by using your own memorabilia and rapid-ageing techniques.

THE VINTAGE LOOK

The vintage look is best described as scruffy and worn, but with an overall sophistication. Vintage features can range from sepia tones or rustic finishes to the rubbed-back or 'distressed' look typical of the feminine 'shabby chic' style.

Rapid-ageing techniques are particularly useful when incorporating new copies of old documents with other items that are more mellow in appearance.

The following techniques can be applied to photos, but do not use originals.

PAPER AND CARDSTOCK

Various techniques can give paper and cardstock a worn look.

Popular methods are paper tearing, paper rolling, paper crumpling and paper scraping (see pages 56–59).

Paper can be sanded lightly with sandpaper or steel wool to remove some of the pattern or highlight creases.

Peel layers off the cardstock or chipboard at the corners or around the edges, leaving some layers loose and curling up to create a worn effect.

CHALKING

Chalking is the most popular technique to age paper and cardstock. Chalk edges after tearing, or chalk the entire piece.

Medium-brown, dark brown and black chalks give the best vintage look. Apply the chalks lightly at first, then add more as needed.

Chalking over the top of crumpled paper or cardstock will add a subtle, mellow look, especially if the creases are emphasized.

PAPER ROLLING

Paper rolling refers to the rolling of a torn edge of paper between the fingertips until it holds itself in a rolled or curled position.

Rolled sections of paper can vary in size and tightness of roll; there are no specific rules on how the roll should look.

Different types of paper will give slightly different effects, but the best papers to use are cardstock or printed paper. Vellum and most other specialty or handmade papers do not roll well.

Space cuts along the paper's edge at uneven intervals, and make sure they do not extend too far into the paper, about 1 cm (^{1}/4 inch). The deeper the cut, the wider the rolled edge.

Some practice may be needed at first to get the rolling action just right. Too much rolling may tear or pill the paper, and too little may cause it to unravel.

ROLLING IDEAS

Once a level of confidence is reached in this technique there are many options for its use.

Tear a hole in the middle of a piece of paper and roll the edges from the inside towards the outside, then place a photo or journalling box behind the paper so it 'peeks' through the hole.

Layer several pieces of rolled paper on top of each other and space them slightly apart so each rolled edge can be seen. Try a beach theme layout with several different shades of blue cardstock to create the effect of waves.

Roll the edges of photo mats and sit the photo inside the rolls. Roll one or more edges of journalling boxes or titles.

Colour or gild the reverse side of the paper before rolling it, so the rolled edges will be a contrasting colour and the rolling technique is accentuated.

PAPER SCRAPING

Paper scraping will only work with cardstock, as paper is not thick enough.

The best method for scraping paper is to hold a piece of cardstock in one hand, with the edges lying straight out in front of you, so the cardstock is horizontal to the floor.

Using one of the blades on a pair of sharp scissors, scrape down the edge of the cardstock, starting at the point furthest away from you and bringing the scissors toward you.

Repeat this over and over until the cardstock starts to become a little 'fluffy' at the edges.

Wipe off the fluff and the result should be similar to the edges of the pages of an old book.

This process is also known as 'knocking' the edges and works particularly well with vintage-style layouts.

PAPER CRUMPLING

Paper crumpling adds texture to the page without being too prominent. Combining the same papers on a layout–but with one crumpled and one left plain–can create an interesting background without the addition of new colours.

Crumpling paper is very easy. It can be done in two ways: dry crumpling and wet crumpling.

For the dry method, just crumple the paper by hand and then unfold and smooth it out. To obtain more wrinkles, repeat the process until the desired effect is achieved.

For wet crumpling, follow the easy step-by-step instructions. This method works best with cardstock, as most patterned papers will disintegrate when wet.

1 Hold the cardstock under gentle running water until wet, or use a spray bottle filled with water to spray the cardstock until it is completely damp.

2 Crumple the cardstock into a ball with your hands. Carefully open your hands to see the creases made and repeat the crumpling if desired. If a small hole should appear, don't worry–this will add to the shabby look.

3 For a rumpled, uneven look, leave the paper to dry naturally. To achieve a flat but still wrinkled effect iron the cardstock while wet or dry, setting the steam option to 'off'. The end result will resemble handmade paper.

Ruth Godden was a beautiful
Bridesmaid at the marriage of her sister
Elsie, to Eric Norman.

WALNUT INK

Walnut ink is made of finely ground walnut shells, and usually comes in crystal form. It is not guaranteed to be acid-free so do not use it directly on photos or allow inked items to come into contact with photos, unless sprayed with a de-acidifying product.

Walnut ink can be used in a multitude of ways. Items can be dunked directly into the ink, or ink can be applied with a soft rag, brush, scrunched-up paper towel or cotton wool ball for different effects. Walnut ink can be sprayed, spattered with a toothbrush or dropped directly on paper.

Experiment on different colours of cardstock. A light wash over pink cardstock makes a lovely antique-rose colour. Vintage fabrics and fibres can be treated with walnut ink. A strong mixture of walnut ink can also be used for writing with a calligraphy pen.

1 Mix the walnut-ink crystals with warm water until they dissolve. Test the strength on the scraps of paper you intend to use, using a small paintbrush.

2 Dip the brush in the walnut ink and lightly cover the paper to tone down the brightness.

3 Repeat the inking process if a darker colour is desired. Leave the paper to dry completely. Add extra depth with chalking and inking if desired.

OTHER AGEING TECHNIQUES

Rubbing edges with metallic rub-ons will give them a gilded look. An unevenly gilded item is perfect for evoking the look of faded grandeur.

Lightly smear or dab an inkpad directly onto the paper, or just to its edges. Applying ink lightly over the top of crumpled paper or cardstock adds extra depth to the overall effect.

When applied sparingly with a dry brush, acrylic paint can give a lovely worn look to patterned paper.

Embellishments can be given the shabby treatment. Sand premade items, such as buttons, wood, metals, stickers and other embellishments. Almost anything can be sanded. Apply acrylic paint to metals or plastics and then wipe off the excess before it dries. This works particularly well with paints that are white, black or verdigris coloured.

COLLAGE

The busy, but organized, look of collage is a popular trend in scrapbooking, especially in heritage albums where its vintage appearance works well. When building a collage-style layout, ensure the design does not overpower the photos.

Larger photos stand out better from the busy background. A number of smaller photos placed in a group can look effective. Generally, one-third of the layout should consist of photographs.

Do not introduce too many colours. Collage is about a merged overall effect rather than any individual item standing out. Shapes and textures will take on extra focus. Use round shapes (such as an optical lens, round page pebble or clock face) to set off rectangular shapes. Use long, thin shapes (twine, ribbons, etc.) to connect and 'ground' items to the layout.

Mix textures by using paper, glass, plastic and metal items together.

Travel

Travel photos are often accompanied by collections of related memorabilia.

By scrapbooking a travel album you can make the most of your special memories.

A box frame is an especially evocative method of preserving and displaying

a colourful collection of travel photographs, postcards and other mementos.

TIPS FOR TOO MANY TRAVEL PHOTOS

If there are too many photographs for one layout, consider the following suggestions:

Scan and reduce the size of some of the photos

Use expanding pages and flip pages to stretch layouts.

Construct a mini accordion-style book and secure it to the page.

Make a pocket for the extra photos.

Scan and store photographs onto a CD which can be included on a layout for easy access.

TRAVEL PHOTOS AND MEMORABILIA

People often dedicate a whole album to a special trip or family vacation, including photos and all kinds of memorabilia.

Items collected on the trip that will help in the recollection of events and places experienced throughout the journey include itinerary, tickets, boarding passes, brochures, hotel receipts, foreign currency, maps and tourist guides.

If travelling regularly, consider creating one album that features the trips in chronological order. If the trip is lengthy an entire album may be necessary to display all the pertinent photographs and memorabilia that have been collected.

Most people would organize their travel album in chronological order. Others may create their album by country, tour itinerary, or highlights of favourite places.

TRAVEL ALBUMS

After unpacking from a trip and settling back into life, make some time to organize your photos and memorabilia. Do not wait too long to complete this task as important details connected with the items may be lost with time.

Once the sorting has been completed, start sketching each layout.

Select the photographs and papers to be used with each layout. The colour of the papers should complement the photos and can at times be selected specifically to recapture the feel of a location.

A box frame is a good way of displaying travel memorabilia. Refer to the section on Memorabilia so you know how to care for any keepsakes.

JOURNALLING

The easiest way to remember the experiences on a trip is to keep a travel diary. Spend time each day recording the highlights and any interesting facts or phrases associated with the location. This will build the foundation for journalling later on, when the album layouts are being completed.

The information from the diary will make the journalling more meaningful as specific details can be recalled.

When journalling, ask for specific accounts or recollections from all family members. This will vary the flavour of the album and provide diverse viewpoints. Often, the younger generation see things differently and this might add a refreshing insight into the photographs.

Other things that are fun to record are the prices of items, foods eaten and unusual local customs.

MEMORY TRIGGERS

Postcards and photographs can assist the journalling process. Taking shots of street and city signs, monument plaques and public transport can trigger memories and help connect them in a layout.

Journalling should include any funny and amusing things that happened on the trip. Photographs are not always necessary to record these moments as the camera is usually tucked away when they occur.

Use travel guides to assist with the journalling as they provide accurate information on places, especially historical sights.

Inclusion of map sections may also help make the connection and highlight the route travelled.

Remember to spray items with a de-acidifying spray before including them in a layout.

EXTRA IMAGES

Postcards purchased when travelling can be a great back-up for photographs. Postcards capture the images that may be missed, such as a view of the Eiffel Tower at night, aerial views of the Grand Canyon, or underwater photos of the Great Barrier Reef.

Postcards also come in handy if the photographs do not develop well. If you arrive home to find that snapshots didn't turn out as well as expected, don't despair. You can scrapbook postcards and other memorabilia, such as pamphlets.

The internet is a great place to find images of the places visited and serves as a source of information for journalling. Several photographs in the Egypt layout were downloaded from the internet, as were the hieroglyphics.

1 Select a 30.5 x 30.5 cm (12 x 12 inch) piece of cardstock to form the bottom of the box frame. Use a scalpel and cutting board to cut four pieces of foam core into strips that are 2.5 cm (1 inch) wide and 30.5 cm (12 inch) long for the sides of the frame.

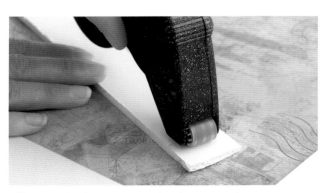

2 Attach the strips to the frame with permanent adhesive squares. Trim off the excess foam core with a scalpel.

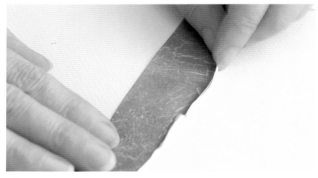

3 Cut out a frame from a 30.5 x 30.5 cm (12 x 12 inch) sheet of printed paper or cardstock. The width should be about 3.8 cm (1½ inches). Attach this paper to the top of the foam core and roll back the inner edges. The foam core should not be visible.

4 Use a hole punch tool, hammer and eyelet setter to set the eyelets throughout the frame bottom. Thread gold cord through to make a crisscross pattern as shown. Tape the cord ends to the back of the page. Add a backing of plain cardstock to hide the cord ends.

5 Form a collage of photos and memorabilia. Attach these with spray glue to the frame bottom, underneath the gold cord. Memorabilia can be sprayed with 'Archival Mist' if desired.

6 Embellish the outer frame with an assortment of travel stickers. Glue stickers to photo mats made from hessian for a handmade look. Use brads and string to emphasize the three-dimensional look.

Babies

One of the most special scrapbooks is a baby album. It records new life entering the world and provides a pictorial account of a baby's first few years. An album offers a means of protecting and displaying treasured photographs and baby memorabilia. The actual compilation of a baby album can be a joyful and rewarding experience in itself.

BABY PHOTOS

Photographs taken at the same time each month will show the baby's growth. Birthdays and holidays also provide special milestones.

Highlight key moments in a baby's life like the first tooth, first table food, first haircut, first-time crawling, first steps and first birthday.

Take close-ups of a baby's face, hands and feet as these features will change quickly and the images can be very effective in a scrapbook layout.

PAPERS AND EMBELLISHMENTS

Many beautiful printed papers and stickers are designed specifically for babies. They are predominantly soft pastels and reflect baby themes such as nursery-rhyme characters.

Embellishments featuring baby clothes and items such as bottles, bibs and nappies can be purchased or easily made. Decorate baby pages with pastel-coloured and gingham ribbon. Buttons help add shape and contrast to a layout.

WHAT TO KEEP

Keep a journal to record the changes that occur each month, including the first time a mother feels the baby move.

Clear pockets can be added to the album to hold memorabilia. Collect ultrasound photographs, baby-shower invitations, hospital ID bracelets, name tags and congratulatory cards.

Once the baby is home, keep special items like the first bib, little booties, a lock of hair, small toys, teething rings and nappy pins.

1 Select the ribbon and cut it into four sections a little longer than double its width.

2 Fold both ends of the ribbon toward the centre, forming a right angle. Protect with a cloth such as a tea towel, then lightly press the ribbon corner with a warm iron.

3 Hold the ribbon corner in place by adding an acid-free adhesive and then securing the corner to the layout.

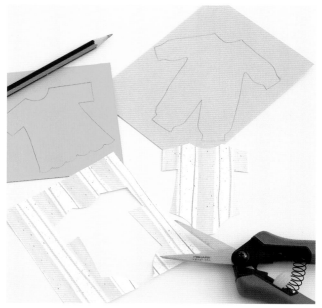

1 This baby gift bag inspired the design of some paper 'baby clothes' which needed to be slightly larger and coloured pink to fit a scrapbook colour scheme. Use the baby clothes patterns in the Patterns section at the back of this book (page 99) and cut them out.

2 Place the patterns on a selection of coloured cardstock. Draw around the templates with a pencil. Cut around the outline with a sharp pair of scissors.

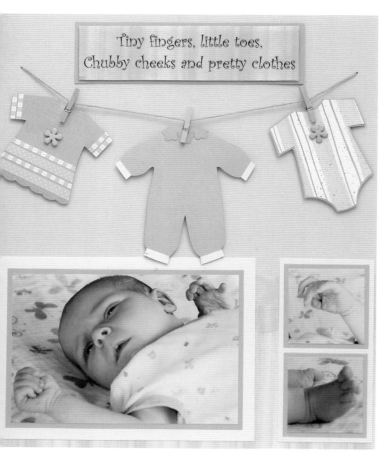

3 Add suitable embellishments, such as these pink eyelets and brads. Attach the cardstock clothes to the layout using tiny pegs and cord.

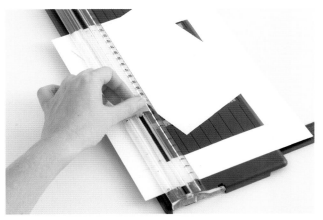

1 Select a textured paper for a photo frame such as this corrugated paper. Mark the photo measurements on the back in pencil and cut out with a paper trimmer.

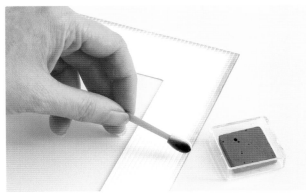

2 Select a darker-coloured chalk that will blend with your layout while creating a 'three-dimensional' effect. Shade the inner and outer edge of the frame with a sponge-tip chalk applicator.

3 Use the numeral stencil or a die-cut numeral and shade the edge with the same-coloured chalk. Leave the chalked elements to set for 24 hours before attaching them to your page.

just the 2 of us

CHALKING TIPS

Choose a chalk colour one or two shades darker than the item to be chalked for definition.

Test on pieces of scrap paper until you get the right amount of colour.

Apply chalk in a circular motion for larger areas, and in a side-to-side motion for edges and thin lines.

Excess chalk or chalk dust should be tapped off the paper, rather than rubbed or flicked away.

Experiment with blending different chalk colours. Always apply lighter colours first then gradually add darker colours in layers, blending the edges with each added layer.

Add definition to the edges of chalked images with acid-free pens or pencils in co-ordinating colours.

Create negative space images by holding a cut-out shape on paper, then chalking around the edges in a light circular motion. Lift the cut-out shape up and its outline will be left on the paper, surrounded by a soft frame of chalk.

Weddings

The style of a wedding album depends on the type of wedding: formal, semi-formal, casual, large, small or intimate. The album should reflect the style and feel of the wedding and provide a way of reliving the experience. Select an album cover that will complement the overall presentation of this very special event.

PHOTO SELECTION

Sort through all the photos, combining professional snaps with those taken by friends. Keep the professional photos intact and try to limit photo cropping.

Decide on a theme for each layout, such as Getting Ready, Bride and Family, Guests and the Reception. Be selective with photos. Each layout should have a focal point–one photo that captures the moment expressed by the overall layout. Surround the focal point with photos that help to support the story.

COLOUR THEMES

As most of the photographs have been taken on the same day, one background colour can be selected to appear throughout the whole album.

Other papers and embellishments could be used from the same colour family or in complementary colours that may bring greater depth to the photographs. Decoration should be sophisticated, subtle and help to complete the layout. Create titles from elegant fonts printed onto matching-coloured papers.

JOURNALLING

Journalling can include how you met, where and how the proposal occurred and the engagement party.

It's important to cover the lead-up to the wedding and some acknowledgement of the stresses of organizing a wedding!

Readers will also appreciate some background on participants such as attendants, witnesses and parents, and their thoughts as well. Lastly, try to recapture and express your feelings on this special day.

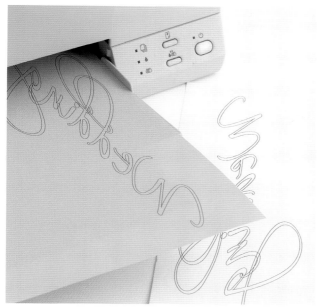

1 Create a title in a text box sized to fit your layout. Style in an appropriate font, such as Scriptina. Format the text so it is reversed (this can be done in Microsoft Word using WordArt). Make a test-copy on plain paper, then print on the actual cardstock.

2 Cut out the heading carefully, using a sharp pair of scissors, nail scissors or a scalpel. Use the printed outline as a guide; it will not be visible when the letter is flipped over.

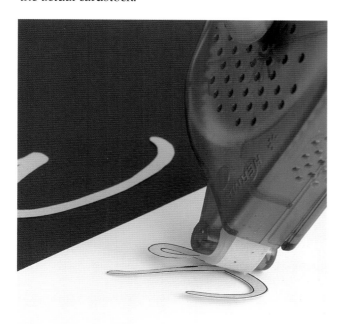

3 Cover the side of the letter that shows the outline with a repositionable adhesive such as Hermafix. Flip the letter over and fix it to the page. Check the original text to determine the spacing between the letters.

Home and garden

Keen scrapbookers develop the habit of scrapbooking everything about their world, such as home life, renovations and the garden. Remember that even seemingly mundane details may interest children or grandchildren in the future. Scrapbooking a garden diary will also provide an attractive guide to planting that the homeowner can use in years to come.

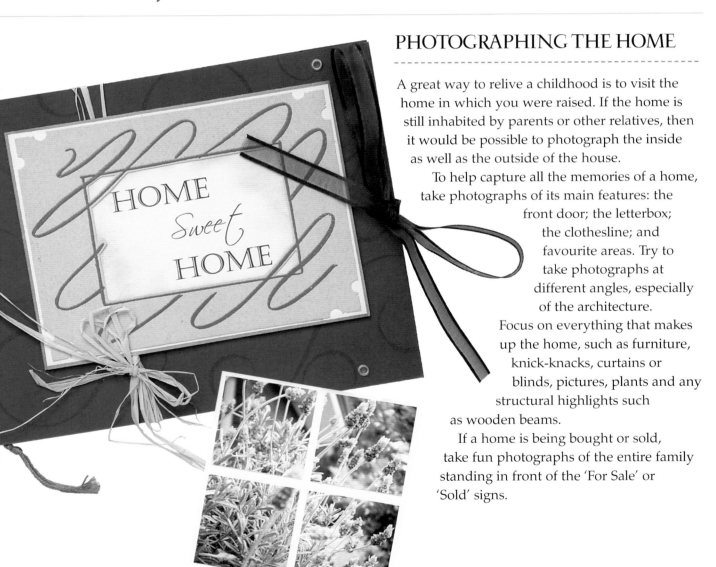

PHOTOGRAPHING THE HOME

A great way to relive a childhood is to visit the home in which you were raised. If the home is still inhabited by parents or other relatives, then it would be possible to photograph the inside as well as the outside of the house.

To help capture all the memories of a home, take photographs of its main features: the front door; the letterbox; the clothesline; and favourite areas. Try to take photographs at different angles, especially of the architecture.

Focus on everything that makes up the home, such as furniture, knick-knacks, curtains or blinds, pictures, plants and any structural highlights such as wooden beams.

If a home is being bought or sold, take fun photographs of the entire family standing in front of the 'For Sale' or 'Sold' signs.

getting the KITCHEN ready

At first glance it seemed we didn't have too much work to do in the kitchen before we moved in... that was until we started measuring things! The fridge was too tall, the microwave too deep and the whole place needed some serious scrubbing.

It took 2 days and nights, 2 large bottles of sugar soap, 3 trips to the hardware store and 8 broken fingernails before that kitchen was ready!!

turn the cupboard into a shelf

extend microwave shelf

Dave removed the cupboard above the fridge, turned it into a large shelf unit and shortened it. With one of the cupboard doors he made an extension for the microwave shelf – voila!

THE HOME ALBUM

Select colours for the layouts that are reminiscent of the particular room or location featured in the photographs. Use fabric from lounge suites, paint from walls and tiles from the kitchen as inspiration for colour choices. Adding fabric and paint swatches in a layout will bring connection and texture to the overall presentation.

When journalling, mention personal details such as why the home is endearing or special to the family, and, if moving, include reasons for this decision.

Mention people such as the neighbours, distances to schools, local shops, parks, work and favourite neighbourhood places. Include a map of the local area somewhere in the album. This will help future generations understand the journalling, especially when referring to schools, local shops or special features in the community.

RENOVATIONS

A common theme in home scrapbooks is renovations. Major home renovations usually represent a considerable personal achievement and investment of time and money. A record of the process will be both emotionally satisfying and useful for showing others.

An effective approach is to simply scrapbook layouts that show before and after photographs.

In the journalling, discuss the time it took to complete, the costs incurred, plans for the renovations and plans for the future.

Local scrapbook stores sell a large range of embellishments that can be used effectively on layouts about the home. Recently, some product lines have based their colour schemes on paint chips used for interior decorating. Using a core colour palette simplifies the process while creating a stunning result.

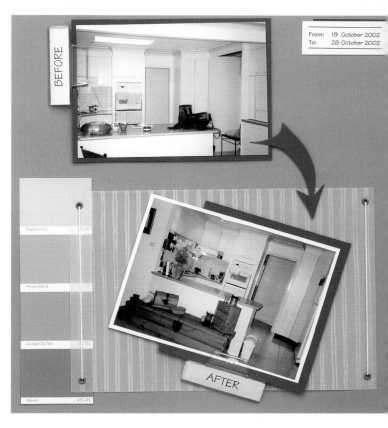

BEFORE

From: 19 October 2002
To: 26 October 2002

Ceylon Ivory

Riviera Sand

Dodge City Tan

Moulin

AFTER

THE GARDEN

The garden is an integral part of the home. Throughout the years, a garden evolves along with the tastes of its caretakers. Photographs, sketches and plant samples can capture the garden's development and can be enjoyed for years to come.

Because of the transient nature of the garden it pays to keep a month-by-month diary with a photographic record of any garden triumphs.

Prized flowers can even be preserved in a scrapbook if they are suitable for pressing.

Create garden planners that record what you planted and where. In time, this will indicate which plants flourish best in the garden and where plants like spring bulbs are due to appear next season.

Garden plans can also help in the future for remembering the name of a rose variety or the year a tree was planted.

WHAT TO KEEP

Gardeners often need to keep scraps of information related to their garden, such as plant tags or the growing instructions on a seed packet. These can rapidly accumulate into an untidy mess.

Clean important seed packets or plant tags carefully. Spray them with 'Archival Mist' to protect any photos included in the layout. Seed packets can also be scanned and printed if you have the equipment.

Preserved flowers, seeds and leaves were featured in scrapbooks during the Victorian era. Old-fashioned methods of flower preservation still work, such as hang-drying flowers or pressing petals in a book or press.

However, flowers for the scrapbook can now be preserved by using a microwave oven (see the step-by-step instructions on page 78) and they can also be laminated with a Xyron machine for extra protection.

DESIGNING GARDEN LAYOUTS

Garden layouts are fun to design and can reflect different gardening styles such as colourful and slightly messy or geometric and orderly.

Shadow-box frames are a great way to protect small items of memorabilia. Use foam core cut out with a scalpel knife to create the raised frame.

An interesting 'window frame' effect (shown in the Spring layout) can be created by photo cropping. Mark a grid pattern on the back of the photograph with a ruler and graphite pencil. Cut along the grid lines with a sharp pair of scissors. Alternatively, make the sections with a square-hole punch.

When sticking the photo pieces to the page, leave an even gap between each piece to make a 'mosaic' design. Do not try this with one-of-a-kind photos.

1 Select well-formed petals or small whole flowers. Wrap the petals or flowers in tissues and place inside a flower press.

2 Place the press (metal press screws must be removed) inside a microwave oven. Weigh down with microwaveable plates. Microwave on high for 20 seconds. Times will vary, depending on the moisture content of the flower.

3 Allow to dry completely before attaching the petals to the layout with a small amount of acid-free craft glue. Petals can also be sealed with craft glue or laminated with a Xyron machine for extra protection.

GARDEN TIPS

These items make wonderful inclusions in a garden scrapbook:

Lightweight garden markers

Scanned or cleaned seed packets

Dried, pressed flowers

Dried seeds and skeleton leaves

Original garden plans

Cuttings from plant catalogues and news-paper or magazine articles

Clear, raised page pebbles

Mosaic-style 'windows'

Raised frames

Floral fabrics

Twine

Garden template pictures

Mini albums

Mini albums and books can be quick to create and make great gifts or keepsakes.

Use them to experiment with new techniques or styles. Mini albums are a good starting

point for a new scrapbooker as a whole album can be completed in just a day or two.

These albums come in a variety of sizes and shapes, including popular tag books.

MINI-ALBUM TIPS

There are plenty of good reasons to create mini albums:

They are quick to plan and complete

You can use up many scraps

You can experiment with new techniques on a smaller scale

You can try a new style that is a departure from your usual taste

You can use up the photos that do not fit on your layouts

ALBUM SHAPES AND SIZES

Premade blank mini albums and books can be purchased from scrapbook stores, ready to be filled with photos and embellishments. These are a good option if time is an issue.

However, the actual construction of a mini album or book is easy, and offers additional options for embellishment before binding the pages together.

There are a few considerations to keep in mind before assembling a mini album or book. Choose a shape that will work best with the theme and the selected photographs; options include square, rectangular or tag shapes.

Tag books make especially good gifts. To make a tag book similar to the one used for 'Travel', follow the step-by-step instructions provided on page 84.

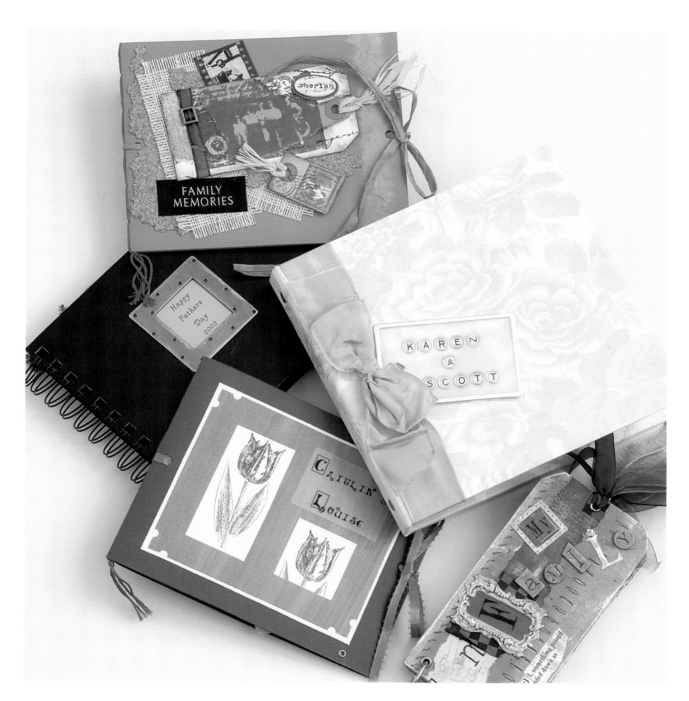

MINI-ALBUM THEMES

Almost any theme is suitable for a mini album. Baby brag books are perfect to keep in a handbag to show off those special baby snaps, or as a gift for a grandparent. Family albums with photos of family members through the years can become treasured keepsakes.

Travel albums with photos, memorabilia and journalling are a quick reminder of a favourite trip.

Wedding albums can show a selection of some of the best photos from a wedding. This makes a wonderful gift for those important anniversaries.

A yearbook is a small pictorial diary of a year in your life. Include everyday photos as well as any special events.

Inspirational albums are a collection of your favourite poetry and quotes. Include some empty pages at the back for future use.

The '10 reasons why' albums are a perfect pocket-sized gift for special occasions such as Mother's or Father's Day (10 reasons why you are the world's best dad or mum); Valentine's Day (10 reasons why I love you); or a friend's birthday (10 reasons why you're my best friend).

Children's personalized storybooks are ideal for the mini-album format. Make up a short story that includes your child and add pictures that go with it. Cut out pictures from old books or magazines, or download them from the internet and print them onto white cardstock. Children love these!

Decide on your theme, then plan the pages in advance so adequate amounts are created. For example, if making a year-in-review album, you may want to allow two pages for each month–one for photos and one for journalling.

COVERS

The mini album can be either hard-covered or soft-covered.

Hard covers are made using chipboard or mat board and are recommended for albums that will be frequently used, such as brag books.

Soft covers are made with cardstock and are perfectly adequate for albums or books that are attached to pages, or not used frequently.

BINDING

Pages can be stitched, stapled or glued together. You can also connect hole-punched pages with hinged rings, twine or waxed linen. Office supply stores also sell a variety of binding systems.

For a really special album, consider having it professionally bound by a printing company that offers this service.

CLOSURES

Mini albums can have a closure at the front or the side. For smaller accordion-style albums that are to be included on a page, closures aren't necessary as the page protector will stop them flying open.

Tag books are usually left without a closure, as they tend to lie or stand reasonably flat.

For larger mini albums some form of closure may be wanted–either for functional or decorative purposes.

Some closures can be complicated, but there are three quick and easy methods. Wrap a length of cotton tape around the album and use a buckle or D-ring to hold the ends together.

Tie ribbon or twine around the album and join it in a bow at the front.

Feed a ribbon through eyelets placed on the edge of the front and back pages and tie it in a bow.

OTHER IDEAS FOR MINI ALBUMS

Mini albums don't have to be stand-alone albums. Very small albums can even be attached to the pages of standard 30.5 x 30.5 cm (12 x 12 inch) albums.

These smaller albums can, for example, hold additional photos that wouldn't otherwise fit on the layout.

If a very small album is to be included on a layout, make sure there is enough room left on the page to attach it, and decide how this will be accomplished.

If it is not too heavy, simply attach the back page of the small album to the scrapbook page with glue.

These small albums can be connected to a layout with threads or ribbon. Punch holes in the layout and feed ribbons through the holes. The ribbons can then be tied to the smaller album.

1 Purchase about 6 to 10 large tags for the actual book pages, and a few smaller tags for layering. Or, make your own tags from cardstock. Choose stamps, papers and stickers that will enhance the selected theme. Stamp a background onto a large tag using a brown dye-based ink pad.

2 Decorate the smaller tags with stamps, photos, and torn journalling. Add dimension and shading by applying chalks in various shades of brown and a touch of black around the edges for definition. Set the small tags aside.

3 Embellish the large tag by alternating layers of torn printed papers and stickers. Torn edges can be chalked for subtle blending. Do not include any bulky items near the left edge as eyelets will be added for assembling the tags into the book.

4 Attach the smaller tag to the larger tag using double-sided adhesive foam. Align all the premade holes with each other. Position this tag over another and poke a pencil through the eyelets to mark a dot on the tag below. This will ensure proper placement of eyelets on each tag.

5 Attach the eyelets to each of the remaining tags where the pencil marks have been made. Attach eyelets to the cover for extra reinforcement. Remaining stickers may be added to the inside covers for continuity and visual appeal.

6 Slide the tags in the correct order (from last page to first) onto two hinged rings fed through the eyelets. Snap the hinged rings closed. Select matching ribbons or fibres to insert through each tag as shown.

Themed albums

A themed album focuses on one idea or subject throughout its pages. Themed albums make unique, wonderful presents that can be frequently revisited and are unsurpassed by commercial items. The homemade look adds an endearing personal quality. The creation of a matching cover is the finishing touch to this one-of-a-kind gift.

SPECIAL THEMES

A well-chosen and presented themed album is a great way to commemorate special occasions or relationships with other people. Popular scrapbook album themes include family, holidays, pets, home renovations, courtships, weddings, sports and hobbies.

A themed album can be created for a birthday or anniversary present. It can be given as a thank-you or in remembrance of a special event, even to help a friend or family member through a difficult time, such as the loss of a loved one.

COVERS

A customized cover is especially appropriate if you are creating a themed album that is intended to be a gift.

Covers that reflect the subjects or themes inside work best, but they don't have to be elaborate. A simple card or motif, even a duplication of one of the internal-page embellishments will work fabulously.

Covers can be decorated with paper or fabric. If the album is subject to frequent handling, add a protective cover made from acid-free plastic.

Every now and then,
Beautiful angels appear
Cleverly disguised
As ordinary human beings...
Mothers!

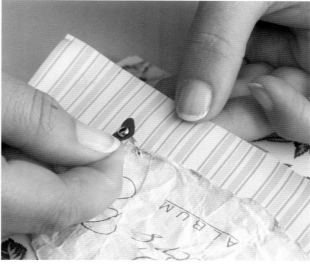

1 Select sheets of extra-thick cardstock to create the album and cover pages. Use background papers and borders that carry your theme through the book. Attach these to the cover.

2 Write or print the album title on co-ordinating cardstock. Embellish with crumpling and chalking techniques. Attach the title to the cover with heart-shaped die-cuts and small brads.

3 When all the pages are completed, punch holes through the left-hand border. Eyelets can be added for extra reinforcement. Tie the album together with co-ordinating ribbons and tassels.

Laying down a hangi for Boxing Day dinner in Muriwai, Poverty Bay.

"Bad to the Axle"

CO-ORDINATING LAYOUTS

Simplicity is the key feature of a themed album and this can easily be accomplished by using the same colours, papers or product range on every layout.

This technique will save valuable time when completing each layout, as many of the design choices in creating a layout are all pre-determined.

The overall layouts can be kept simple, uncluttered, yet effective.

Some co-ordinating embellishments can be used throughout the album to add a personal touch or further emphasize the theme. Examples of embellishments include the small heart-shaped die-cuts added to the brads on the Mother's Day album cover (shown on the previous page).

JOURNALLING

There are many ways to structure the layouts for a themed album. The easiest way is to cover different events as they happened chronologically. However, many other options can be explored with pleasing results.

Creating layouts based on different viewpoints is an entertaining yet personal approach; for example, a Mother's Day album could be based on what a mum means to each of her children.

For a sophisticated, contemporary approach, minimal journalling will draw more attention to the design and the photographs.

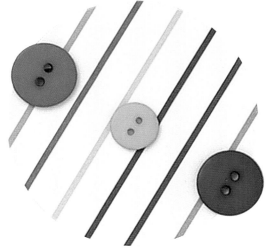

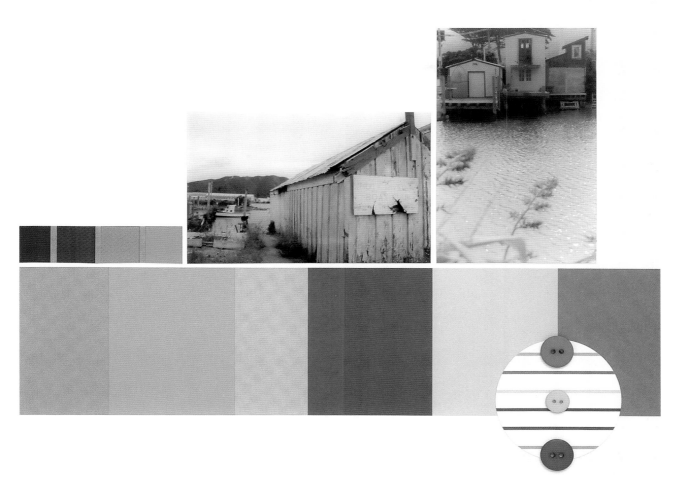

PHOTOGRAPHS

Photographs from personal collections and hobbies can form the basis of a classic themed album.

The layouts on these pages were created using a collection of photos from a photographer's portfolio. The photos tell the story so effectively that little or no journalling is required. The overall design of the layouts enhances the photographs by keeping them as the central focus.

The placement of the photographs mimics the design of the paper.

Embellishments capture an element from the photographs, as seen in the layout, 'Bad to the Axle'.

This album is a great example of less is more.

About me!

Most family photographers find themselves behind the lens so often that they forget to make an appearance in their own albums. Scrapbookers also need to be reminded that besides photographing, journalling and embellishing the experiences of other people they should have some 'about me' space too.

ABOUT ME TIPS

Things to include in your album:

Everything and anything to do with You

Likes and dislikes, beliefs and values

You as a child, a teen, adult, parent, partner, etc.

Childhood, including school, friends, toys and pastimes

Career, including past and current jobs, work-mates, bosses, income and future career goals

ABOUT YOU

An 'about me' album is an album based solely on the individual who creates it. It should encapsulate items from the past, plans for the future and hopes and dreams. The photographs should range from childhood to the present and include significant people in your life.

A great reason for creating an 'about me' album is to leave a legacy that will be read and cherished for generations to come.

JOURNALLING

'About me' albums can be completed in stages; however, it helps to keep a diary and record of any important details and emotions as they happen.

Use 'backwards journalling' as a starting point for a layout. Decide what to say first, then find photos or memorabilia that support the point.

Shy journallers can make use of hidden journalling devices such as envelopes, tags, lift-up flaps, small booklets, or a CD included on the layout.

1 Select an accordion-style 'gang' tag. Write your journalling on the inside pages of the tag.

2 Chalk both sides using medium-brown and red chalks. Add some mini-photos if desired.

3 Decorate the front cover and attach string to the back page for a tie-closure (the back page will be hidden as it is fixed to the layout).

METAL TIPS

A wide range of metal accents and embellishments is available for scrapbooking. Metal can be used in the background, as with metal sheets and metal mesh. It can be purely decorative, as with pages embellished by small metal charms.

Text is available in the form of metal alphabets, words, plaques, bookplates, tags and tiles.

Metals frames, photo corners and hinges can be used to hold photographs. The construction of a page also makes use of metal elements such as conchos, clips and other connectors, the most common being brads (split pins) and eyelets.

Eyelets come in many shapes, sizes and colours. They can be ornamental or used to anchor elements to a layout. Fibres, wire and twine can be threaded through the eyelet holes for added texture.

1 Sand the metal frame with a fine-grade sandpaper to prepare the surface for proper adhesion of the paint.

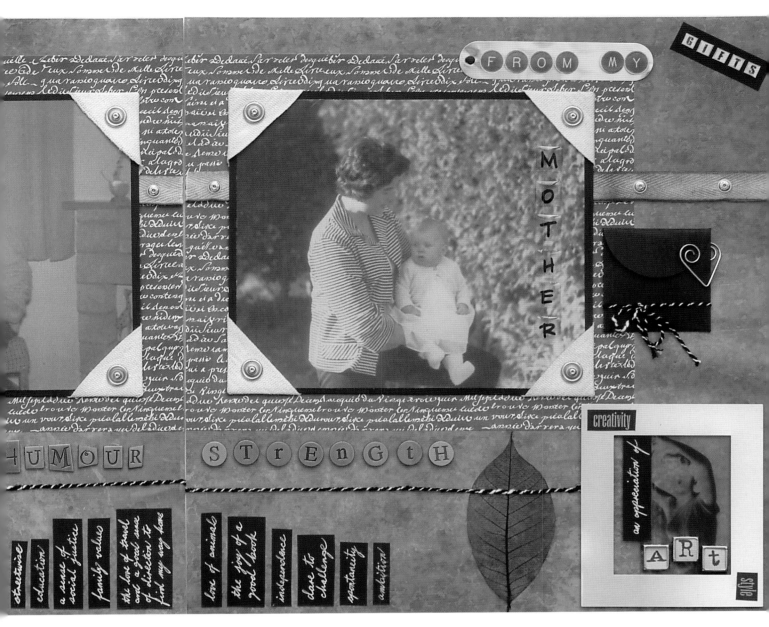

FROM MY

GIFTS

MOTHER

HUMOUR   STRENGTH

creativity

an appreciation of

ART

style

2 Prepare some thick white paint in a small cup or shallow dish without adding water. Paint the frame with a thin coat of paint using a brush or applicator.

3 Leave the painted frame to dry overnight. For added dimension, create a dark edge around the frame with an ink pad.

Scrapbooking for kids

Kids not only enjoy looking through completed scrapbooks but love participating too. Children as young as four years old have the ability to complete scrapbook layouts about their daily life. Scrapbooking together can be an illuminating experience as you glimpse the world from a child's perspective.

WHEN TO BEGIN

The great thing about scrapbooking is that every member of the family can participate. Basic motor skills, especially cutting and pasting, are the foundation.

If a child shows a genuine interest in the craft, try to invest some time with him or her. Demonstrate the correct way to use the tools and discuss some basic design principles. Provide some practice and, above all, let the child be free to try new things. The end product may not be appealing at first but, with time and practice, the quality will improve.

EQUIPMENT

Purchase a small selection of age-appropriate tools and supplies, such as a small paper trimmer, a few decorative (child-friendly) scissors, easy-to-use adhesive, coloured gel pens and stickers, including letters.

Save leftovers scraps from past layouts for the kids to use. It will minimize costs and provide them with a wide choice of papers. They will also enjoy using the same papers seen in other albums.

WHAT TO INCLUDE

Include a child's writing, paintings and drawings in their scrapbook album, but do use a de-acidification spray on any non-acid-free papers. Photos of very bulky artwork are an effective substitute.

Older children may want to try their own photography and a disposable camera is a great way to start them off.

Creating an ABC album will help teach the alphabet and extend vocabulary. Older children love creating ABC albums for younger siblings and this type of album is a potential family heirloom.

1 Use the stencil template in the back of this book. Flip it over and trace each letter shape on to a piece of felt with a felt-tip pen.

2 Cut the letter out with a sharp pair of scissors. As the pen marks are on the reverse side of the felt they will not show when the letter is glued to the matting.

3 Use craft glue to stick the letter to matting made from torn cardstock. Set up an ABC album with one letter of the alphabet on each page. Get the kids to scrapbook any words, stickers, photos or drawings that start with that letter.

Leftover scraps

As beautiful and creative layouts begin to fill a scrapbook, a large collection of leftover papers and notions will begin to accumulate. Scrapbookers are naturally inventive in using up leftover scraps. Cast-off items can be transformed into stunning creations, either for a scrapbook or for other uses.

ORGANIZING SCRAPS

The most important element when conserving is organization. Like other scrapbook supplies, the leftovers are best separated into solids and patterns, then arranged in colour groupings.

Small, clear, expanding folders work well for this and can be purchased at scrapbook or office supply stores.

Remember to use only acid-free storage components and store them in a cool, dry location away from direct sunlight.

EMBELLISHMENTS

Notions and other embellishments can be kept in one location to prevent them from getting lost or forgotten.

Sometimes, spotting a collection of notions in a storage tray will spark off ideas for future creations.

New embellishments for a layout can easily be made with leftovers. They can be torn, aged, rolled, punched, stamped, embossed, printed and combined to create the right accent for any project.

LEFTOVER CREATIONS

Leftover materials can be used to make beautiful cards, bookmarks, CD-holders, mini-books, placecards, journalling blocks, frames, collages and paper-piecing projects.

Just as quilters use fabric scraps to create a masterpiece, paper quilts can be created for a beautiful background on any scrapbook layout.

Utilizing the leftovers will help make the best use of a scrapbooker's investment and keep the spirit of innovation alive.

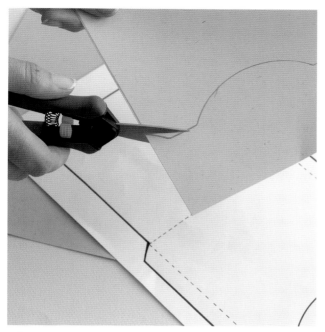

1 Enlarge the CD-cover pattern in the Patterns section of this book (page 98) on a photocopier by 150%. Trace the pattern onto a piece of leftover plain cardstock. Cut out the cardstock along the solid lines.

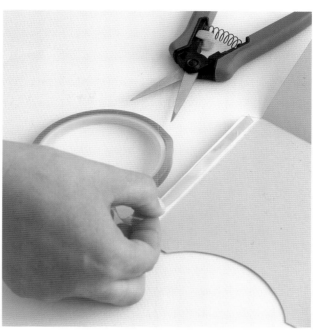

2 Score along the dotted lines on the cardstock, then fold the flaps inwards. Fix the sides of the CD cover together with double-sided tape.

3 Decorate the CD cover as desired using leftover scraps and embellishments. For this cover the scraps were torn and then fastened with brads and eyelets.

CD cover

CD Cover for the 'Leftover scraps' project on pages 96–97.

Enlarge this pattern on a photocopier by 150%.
Note that solid continuous lines are cutting lines and dotted lines are fold lines.

Baby clothes

Baby clothes for the 'Babies' project on pages 69–70.

Photocopy this pattern at 100%.

Project makers

This edition published in 2005 by Bay Books
an imprint of Murdoch Books Pty Limited
Pier 8/9 23 Hickson Road Sydney
NSW 2000
Phone: +61 (0) 2 8220 2000
Fax: +61 (0) 2 8220 2558

Murdoch Books UK Ltd
Erico House, 6th Floor North
93/99 Upper Richmond Road
Putney, London, SW15 2TG
Phone: +44 (0) 20 8785 5995
Fax: +44 (0) 20 8785 5985

Editor: Anouska Jones
Designer: Nanette Backhouse, saso content & design
Photographer: Ian Hofstetter
Stylist: Anne-Maree Unwin
Authors: Frank Saraco; Louise Riddell
Additional Text: Joanne Green; Leanne Hand
Scrapbooking Consultants: Joanne Green; Leanne Hand; Louise Riddell; Frank Saraco
Template Design and Illustration: Spatchurst
Additional Illustration: Tricia Oktober; Tracy Loughlin; Isn't She Clever Design and Illustration
Production: Megan Alsop

National Library of Australia Cataloguing-in-Publication Data

Riddell, Louise.
Scrapbooking projects.

ISBN 0 681 06689 X.

1. Paper work. 2. Paper work - Patterns. I. Saraco, Frank.
II. Title.

745.54

Printed by Sing Cheong Printing Company Ltd. PRINTED IN CHINA.
First printed in 2005.
© Text, photography, design and illustrations
Murdoch Books Pty Limited 2005.

Acknowledgements
The publisher would like to thank the following for supplying products for photography:
Scrapbook Cottage, 2/8 Victoria Avenue, Castle Hill NSW 2154, www.scrapbookcottage.com.aue Hill NSW 2154, www.scrapbookcottage.com.au

Circle template

Oval template

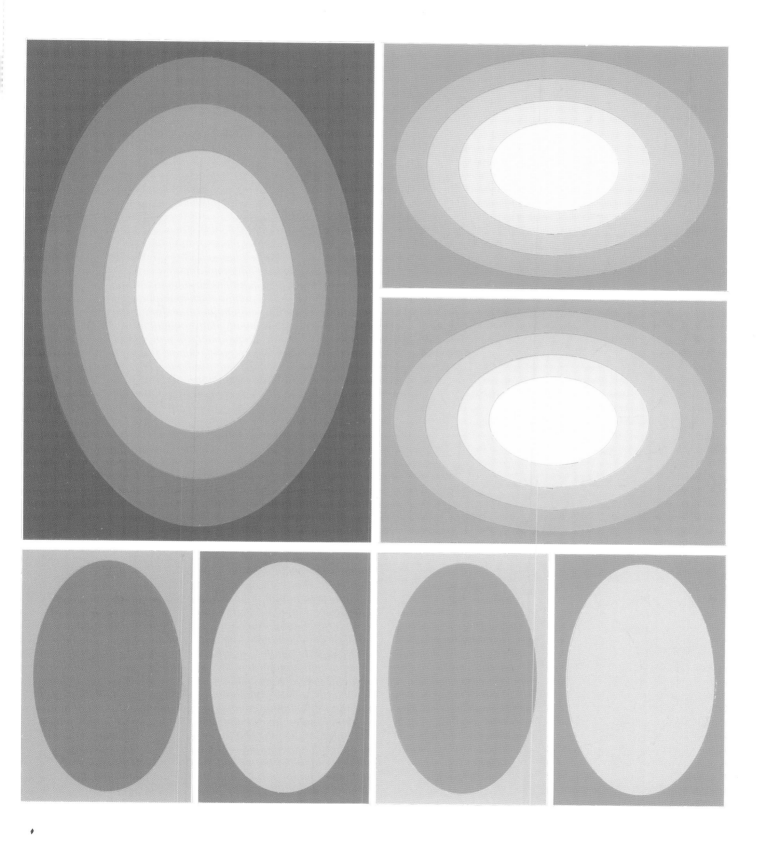

Uppercase stencil

A B C D E F
G H I J K L
M N O P Q
R S T U V
W X Y Z ? !

Lowercase stencil

abcdefg
hijklmn
opqrstu
vwxyz?!

Uppercase letters

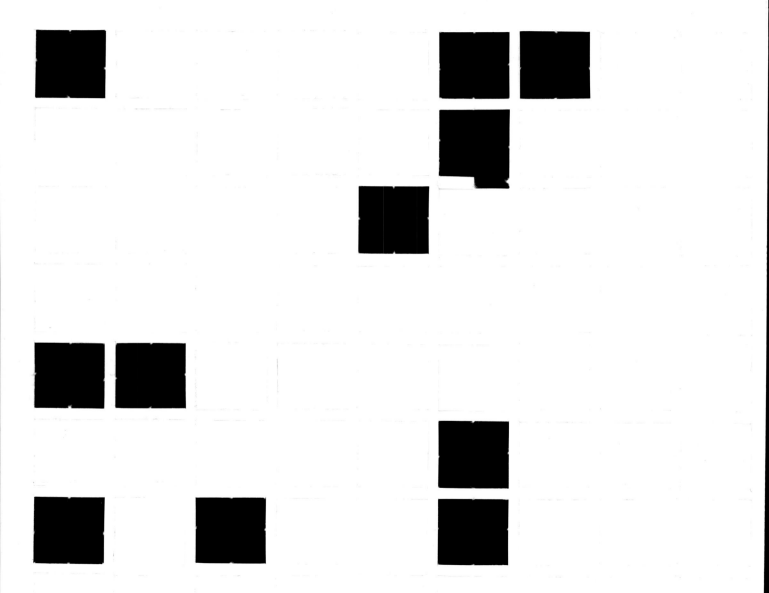

Lowercase letters

a	a	a	a	b	b	b	c	c
c	d	d	d	e	e	e	e	f
f	f	g	g	g	h	h	h	i
i	i	i	j	j	j	k	k	k
l	l	l	m	m	m	n	n	n
o	o	o	o	p	p	p	q	q
q	r	r	r	s	s	s	t	t
t	u	u	u	v	v	v	w	w
w	x	x	x	y	y	y	z	z
.	.	¨	'	,	^	ç	?	!

Numbers

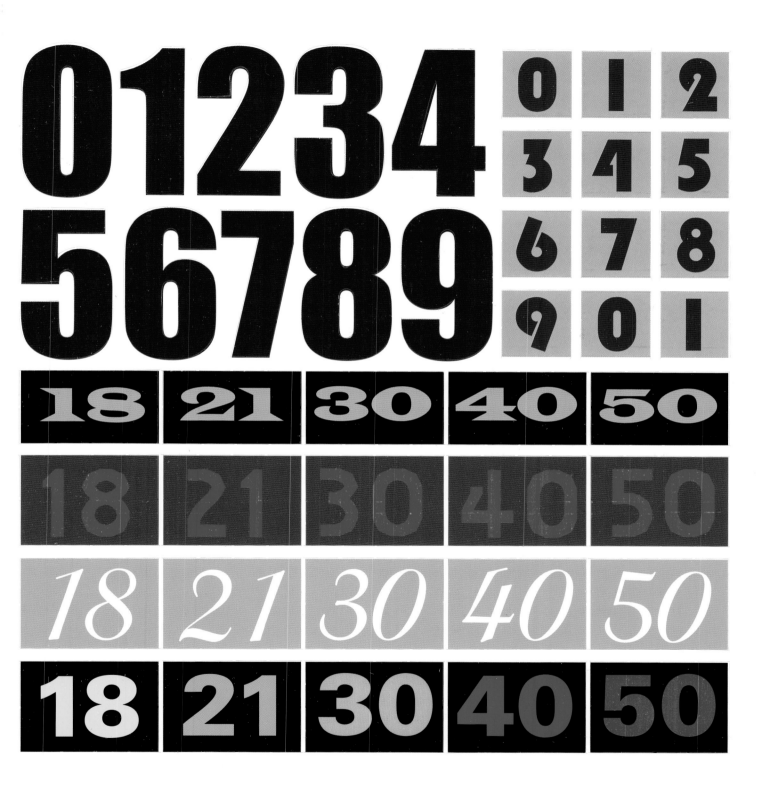

Baby frames

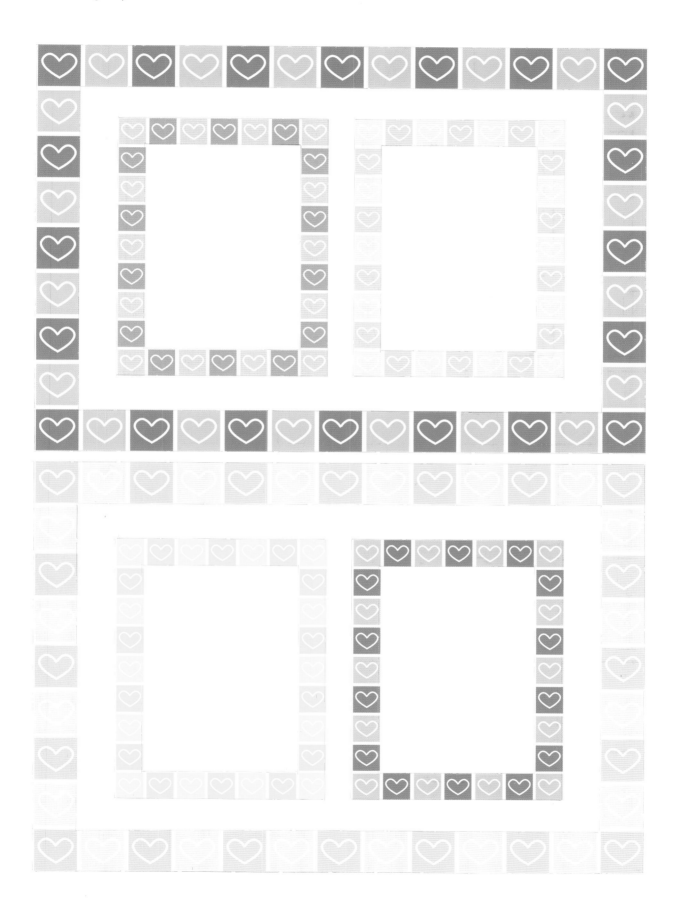

Borders

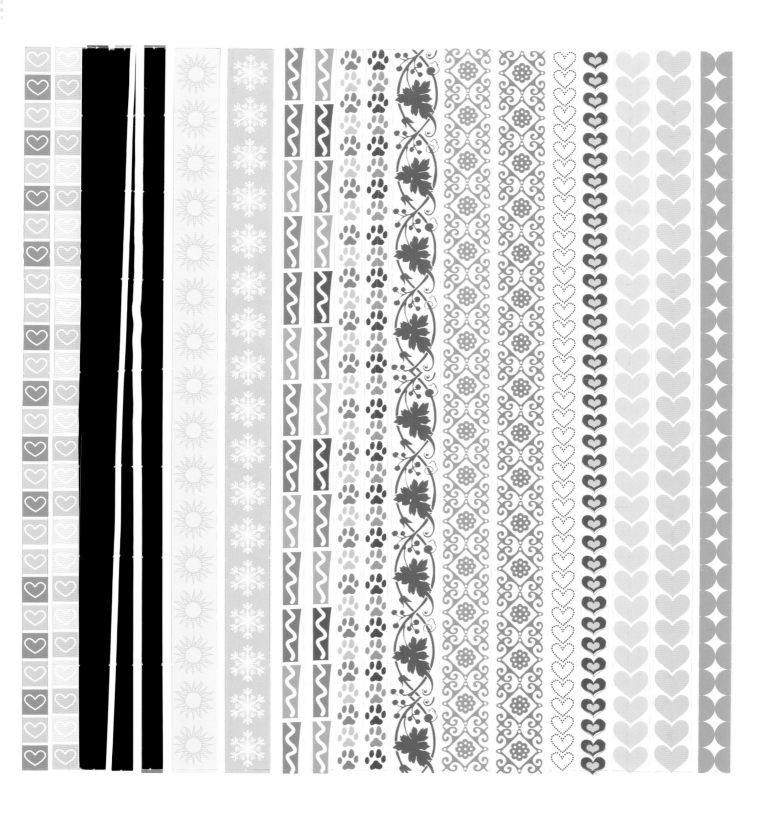

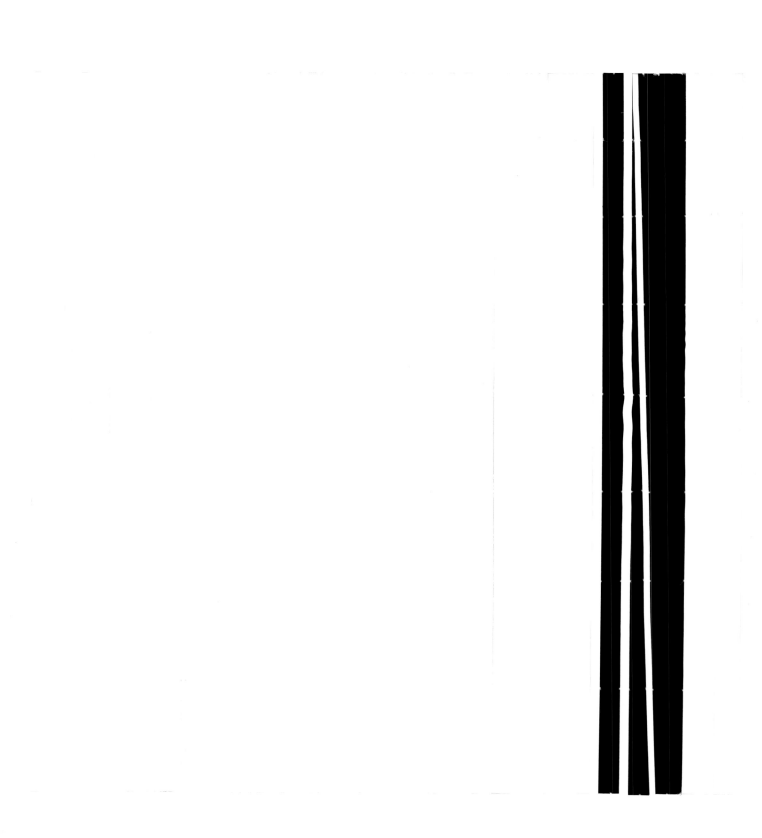

Babies

Romance

Activities